Bost

Boston

Edited by
Paul S. Rowe

Dostoyevsky Wannabe Cities
An Imprint of Dostoyevsky Wannabe

First Published in 2020
by Dostoyevsky Wannabe Cities
All rights reserved
© All copyright reverts to individual authors

Dostoyevsky Wannabe Cities is an imprint of
Dostoyevsky Wannabe publishing.

www.dostoyevskywannabe.com

This anthology is a work of fiction. The names, characters and incidents portrayed in it are the work of the authors' imagination. Any resemblance to actual persons, living or dead, events or localities is entirely coincidental.

Cover design by Dostoyevsky Wannabe

ISBN-9798625817004

Dostoyevsky Wannabe Cities books represent a snapshot of the writing of a particular locale at a particular moment in time. The content is reflective of the choices of the guest-editor.

No parts of this publication may be reproduced, stored in a retrieval system, or transmitted in any form or by any means, electronic, mechanical, photocopying, recording, or otherwise, without the prior written permission of the copyright owner.

This book is sold subject to the condition that it shall not, by way of trade or otherwise, be lent, resold, hired out, or otherwise circulated without the publisher's prior consent in any form of binding or cover other than that in which it is published and without a similar condition including this condition being imposed on the subsequent purchaser. Under no circumstances may any part of this book be photocopied for resale.

This book is dedicated to the loving memory and
noble spirit of the philosopher-poet
Ifeanyi Menkiti

Contents

Ed Simon	11
Peter Caputo	23
Susan Rich	37
Ruth Lepson	43
Sassan Tabatabai	47
Philip Nikolayev	53
Raquel Balboni	59
Fanny Howe	65
Ben Mazer	69
Wyatt Bonikowski	99
Meagan Masterman	107
Maria Pinto	117
Jenny Grassl	129
Peter Brown	135
James Stotts	147
Susan Barba	157
George Kalogeris	167
Tope Ogundare	177
Fred Marchant	185
Jennifer Barber	189
George Saitoh	197
Meia Geddes	221
Liz Sux	235
Pınar Yaşar	241
Elke Thoms	247

Stephen Sturgeon	253
Nate Klug	259
Stephanie Burt	265
Cassandra de Alba	271
Sarah O'Brien	277
Katia Kapovich	285
Ryan Napier	289
Porsha Olayiwola	299
Contributors	305

Ed Simon

City on a Hill: Redux

"I'm in love with Massachusetts."
— Jonathan Richman and the Modern Lovers

About 450 miles south of Boston, at 8th and F Streets NW in the Old Patent Office Building, there is a white-walled gallery which is the first room amongst an exhibition designated with the lofty title of "American Origins." Hanging near paintings of worthies like John Smith and Pocahontas is an amateurish portrait of that demon-haunted founder of Massachusetts—John Winthrop. The portrait is an early nineteenth-century copy of an original made from Winthrop's likeness, before he boarded the *Arbella* at Yarmouth, Isle of Wight in 1630, and made that three-week pilgrimage across cold North Atlantic waters to an imagined refuge in that place which had formerly been called Virginia, but which had recently been rebaptized as a "New England."

Whether the original was more proficient in its accuracy is hard to say; the copier of Winthrop's portrait has attempted a likeness that bears some similarity to paintings of the late Renaissance, with its subject posed in a Jacobean collar of delicate lace and a fashionable Dutch-style van Dyke that has grown out thickly, as if prepared for the chill of a trans-Atlantic voyage. Winthrop's skin is waxy and grey, his auburn hair long and parted in the middle like Christ's, his eyebrows thick and wryly arched, and the slight indications of a smile (or a sneer?) upon those thin lips. An undistinguished oil painting of two by three feet, no doubt made for historical posterity rather than aesthetic appreciation, and otherwise completely forgettable, save for one detail. What is most arresting about the portrait is Winthrop's strange and cracked gaze.

Whoever created the portrait saw fit to depict Winthrop with almost completely black eyes. His pupils expand out nearly to the corners, the white of his sclera almost totally obscured in an obsidian finality. Like two, wide, coal-black absences – lacuna in the orbitals of the Puritan divine. As if want of light in the darkened sanctuary of some white-washed Suffolk chapel, or in the bowls of the *Arbella,* or amongst the dread December blackness of a Massachusetts errand into the wilderness, had expanded his pupils out to the very edge of his lids. Combined with that smile, the portraitist has made Winthrop downright horrifying. Strange, eerie, uncanny, chilling, inhuman. Eyes that are blackholes, eyes that have seen everything that has happened, and everything that is to come. Every broken promise, every violated covenant. These are alien eyes. These are God's eyes.

Winthrop was, of course, a zealous Calvinist who wished to purify the Church of England of all of its superstitious popery and so would establish a Godly republic in the American wilderness. As the anonymous portrait's fashions make clear, this founder of

Massachusetts was very much a child of the Renaissance. Born the year Spain's Armada threatened England and dead the year Charles I would be decapitated, a man closer to the medieval than to the architects of American Federalism who'd found the city where his official portrait now hangs. Charter of the colonial shock troops of the Puritan Great Migration that would ultimately finish the evil task of genocide against the natives which European pilgrims had started generations before. Arriving a full decade after the more famous Pilgrims had similarly set out for New English shoals, and Winthrop doesn't feature in our more cliched American Stations of the Cross—he wasn't at the first Thanksgiving and he was dead long before those girls martyred as witches by Salem. But in all of his roiling, difficult, black-eyed contradictions, he's arguably among the first of Americans—with all that that implies.

I don't mean to be cruel to Winthrop, who like the other Puritans I spent the better part of a decade studying in graduate school. Despite his sins, Winthrop was, in some ways, an admirable governor of the Massachusetts Bay Colony. I've developed an odd affection for him. Some of the contraries we see in the American character are so obvious in him; the religious theocrat who advocated for socialism. The zealous Puritan who was still willing to warn a liberal friend that he needed to escape to what would be Rhode Island, and thus prevented Winthrop's fellow officials from arresting

Roger Williams. A pragmatist squeezed by John Endicott to the right and Henry Vane to his left, Winthrop dispensed his office with all the moderation that one can imagine a Puritan as dispensing. He maintained the colony's interactions with the natives to some degree of humanity, even if he ultimately shares in that collective responsibility for the tragedy bloodily forced upon them.

In addition to being humane and loving, Winthrop could be dogmatic, fundamentalist, cruel. His conduct in the so-called Antinomian Controversy was despicable, when sainted Anne Hutchinson was persecuted for her heresies (not least of which was being a woman willing to teach scripture). Whatever the merits of the historical man, Winthrop isn't his own, however. He's moved into that eternal realm of American myth and symbol, and has come to signify something much larger than simply being another founder of Massachusetts. Winthrop is seen as the originator of an idea, he who dreamed of a veritable "Empire of Liberty," the mayor of his own City on a Hill.

Anachronistic to see Winthrop as some sort of partisan of American freedom in the seventeenth-century, and yet his endlessly quoted, misquoted, alluded towards line from the sermon "A Modell of Christian Charity," which he supposedly delivered on the *Arbella,* is what most remains of the man, while his bones have long since turned to dust in the King's Chapel Burying Ground off of Tremont. "For we must consider that we shall be a city upon a hill," Winthrop read aloud in his lay-sermon to an audience who would instantly catch the reference to the book of Matthew. "The eyes of all people are upon us," (especially unforgiving coal-black ones) "so that if we shall deal falsely with our God in this work we have undertaken," (and really, who doesn't in the end deal falsely with God in the work that they've undertaken?) "and so cause Him to withdraw his present help from us, we shall be made a story and a byword through the world." America, built upon one giant Indian burial ground and mustered into existence with a warning and a curse whispered aboard a ship by a Puritan barrister. The line is often read as optimistic.

The museum in which Winthrop's likeness hangs, Washington DC's National Portrait Gallery, is a twentieth-century attempt to do what American historiography has always done—to impose a little bit of narrative coherence on a story that often has none. Suddenly the figures who populated sixteenth and seventeenth-century America—Algonquin and Iroquois, Abenaki and Narraganset, enslaved women and men of the Wolof and the Ibo, colonists from Spain, France, Sweden, the Netherlands, and England, are all repurposed into a story where the foregone conclusion is "The United States of America." Winthrop figures in that story as the prophet of American exceptionalism; a man who could see beyond the internecine, sectarian squabbles of a dozen different varieties of "hot Protestantism" and somehow understand that what they were attempting on the Massachusetts' shore was bigger than parliamentary debates in an England on the verge of revolution, bigger even than the godly job of reforming the Church.

Whether accurate to his views or not, Winthrop's allusion to the beatitudes, his City of God in the American wilderness, has dogged our sense of identity ever since. The providential nation, the elect nation. Two roads lead to Winthrop's city on a hill; one goes through that rock in New York Harbor on which the Mother of Exiles stands, the other through a very different region, "strategic hamlets" in Vietnam incinerated by napalm, dusty villages on the Tigris and Euphrates shelled with ironically named Tomahawk missiles. If Winthrop is an American founder, then in that exceptionalism he supposedly extoled he is the equal founder of two different Americas.

Historians don't know when Winthrop delivered his sermon; it may have been on the *Arbella,* perhaps on the docks in southern England. While it was passed around in manuscript form for centuries, it didn't see publication well into the nineteenth-century, a convenient little axiom for the murderous Manifest Destiny of Jacksonian democracy. In the twentieth-century, as "American Studies" established itself as its own discipline (often times with money from the State Department or the CIA), historians like Perry Miller, F.O. Mathieson, Leo Marx, R.W.B. Lewis, and Henry Nash Smith helped to construct a particular model of American identity—founded in New England by Puritans, defined by Protestant intellectual commitments which then secularized into sober, industrious American democracy and capitalism, extending from Boston out to the Pacific and conveyed through symbolic language. The Frontier. The Errand into the Wilderness. The City on a Hill.

Many of the Puritans did see their mission to America in specifically millennial terms, as the potential establishment of a "New Jerusalem" at the ends of the world which would prefigure the coming apocalypse and the perfect reign of Christ. As a principle of American exceptionalism, it's stripped of the theological gloss, ostensibly secularized while we recall that the original formulation has its own tinge of heresy about it as well, moving scriptural drama from the Holy Land into New England. A tremendous self-regard in the phrase, where his warning is completely obscured in the many subsequent quotations of Winthrop, his words in the mouths of John F. Kennedy, Ronald Reagan (who made the "city on a hill" a "shining beacon," like some casino), Barack Obama.

Better to remember the full impact of what he said; that if there is a covenant which is implied in the idea of America, its abandonment will only bring ruin. Lest Winthrop simply be seen as a triumphal chauvinist, recall what exactly the covenant of the City on a Hill was, for true to his title, he declaims that "We must delight in each other, make each other's conditions our own, rejoice together, mourn together, labor and suffer together, always having before our eyes our commission and community in the work, our community as members of the same body." No wonder the eyes of the world are upon us, judging us.

The "City on a Hill" is a metaphor of course; the real Boston isn't particularly hilly, at least not to a native Pennsylvanian such as myself. Still, a sacredness to the actual place, the uncanny sense that what was built here, purchased in their own oppressions and in the unwilling blood of others on a peninsula that the natives called Shawmut, was in some sense a New Jerusalem. An ambivalence in that covenant, as contradictory as Winthrop's character which exiled Hutchinson and saved Williams. The moment you try and establish Utopia then it has already failed of course; such is the nature of the project. Perhaps New Jerusalem was a real place for an instant in the glint of a black eye; maybe Boston was such a place before it was ever founded, in the second that Winthrop collectively imagined it with his audience. "The land was ours before we were the land's," as Robert Frost put it.

Hard to see the actual city, charming as Boston may be, as the celestial metropolis dropped from heaven unto the Atlantic coast. Red-bricked Cambridge with its maddening one-way streets; touristy Faneuil Hall, and bucolic Boston Common, cement gritted Southie and tree-lined Brookline—they're many things, but it's not exactly the mystical, apocalyptic, millennial city of Winthrop's imagination. And yet…. how can we not see traces of that dream, at least by the virtue of the fact that *this is the actual place where they tried to establish that New Jerusalem?* In his contradictions and inconsistencies, Winthrop is truly the most American of founders; and in its contradictions and inconsistences Boston is the most American of cities.

The Puritan metropolis permeated with secularity, the abolitionist capital whose racism remains lamentably thick, the cosmopolitan Athens of America and the provincial town. All of America revels in contradiction, but maybe Boston a little more so. It's hard not to find it beautiful; it's hard not to fall in love with whatever utopia may have been embodied by Massachusetts, while understanding that the actual Utopia, as forever, must always be submerged beneath a wave just a bit further to the west, onward and onward. Looking into Winthrop's eyes long enough, you realize that across that chasm of time he's looking right back at you, as if to remind his viewer that America has been composed of many New Jerusalems, but Boston was the first. His eyes are upon us.

Peter Caputo

Her Lady Nameless

I

The long black hair, dark eyes unknown. On the Fifty-Seventh Street Station she carried the history of my grief.

Here is a birth and we rejoice in the story that begins with a simple truth. It was light rain that sent him below. There on the uptown subway station he saw her, young and lovely, but unfamiliar. In her eyes was the history of his grief.

In those dark eyes all the losses I had ever known. What was she doing with the women so plain, so pretty, the graceful and coarse, the saintly and cruel, women who somehow knew when I could not that all they would ever give were trinkets, tinsel to me and handsome gifts to my memory? What was this history of lost love in her black eyes and how could she be of this world and who is she to take my things?

What more to be said of her eyes, the history of love in her eyes? His history is carried in the eyes of another, his pain calling to him from the depths of another's iris. A stranger's eyes can hold your past like crystals and jewels. Eyes are among the many things we know, for Guardians are little else but sight. Caretakers of all plots ignited by the Nameless, we burn with the most distant stars when characters are born. Our eyes watch them grow as we move and guide the stories into which they slide. This heavy-eyed woman, what else could she be but of his world?

And my dreams I saw dancing in her eyes, all those losses that have made their way into my uneasy sleep. Rooftop saxophones whistling the sun off city monuments and the makeup off the plain and pretty women in rush hour trench coats, the worm beneath their heels tempting them to begin again, sell bad apples to young men, and foul the cathedrals of the old and the crippled. The microscopic sketch of a hand holding a pen at the bottom of a blank page on my basement floor, the manhole to somewhere I needed to be, the howling wolves in Riverside Park who raise the city from the dead each morning. If dreams too were in her eyes, why? What could she do with dripping nightmares, this dark-eyed lovely who wouldn't know a nightmare if her eyes were made from night, if the shine of her fresh face and halo burned themselves to grime?

In life, in dreams, losses are one to her. She knows that lost loves live many lives and the three-dimensional reappears in the night under a fluttering sky. Living love becomes dream love with high-pitched saxophones and things in trench coats. These are one to her, his life and dreams. And halos? There is no halo, just a character made for such a story.

The people she stole too, the things that mingle with loss as I stumble over the moments of each day, she stole these, the many shop clerks and subway riders watching me in ridicule, the hands of their contempt reaching through my chest to tease a swollen heart, the clock on my kitchen wall keeping pace with my melancholy pulse, never the right time, always a life, and even the tall man on the other side of the mirror, he who greets me with shaved head and yellow teeth that stink through glass, the yellow man was there. There in her eyes was the grief I've streaked across the world, all my losses that change shape as I breathe in and out. She held my maudlin fantasies, the pathetic victim with his murky assailants. She stole the things I would have no one see. That's the on-screen world, isn't it? All that is hidden unveiled, my foolish head emptied for the one-penny crowd. How sickening that anyone would want the silent ghosts of a skinny man. The world is full of dark spirits, ugly and menacing, spewing their viscous sins onto mountains and seas. Let her take them if she must steal.

It is only loss she carries. Living in flesh or dreams or among the clocks and mirrors of his fear and fantasy, loss remains what is. The dark eyes of the unfamiliar woman draw no lines. She carries his grief, that's all.

I would howl if the moon would let me. Watching the sky I know the reason I am not a man but a spiritless wailing wolf. Lift my grief and my soul goes with it but how can I cry thief when so much is missing? The souls of houses and weddings, children and song, blessings and departure. And the moving, mumbling bones attached to wires and waves, dead for the price of a microchip. She's taken my soul but who am I to complain in this life, this vacuum we call fullness.

Soulless is only another form of life. Walk with body, go without soul. Could he imagine the purity in this? Could he know that even the vampires are pure and the wolves that follow them? Let him move through his story now.

All night I've been up thinking of those spacious eyes. What is that wide expanse within if not hell? The Devil takes your soul but in her eyes is no fire of hate. What is the space that hosts your soul but is not hell? What is this place that has my things and does it sprout the trees that made a blank page in a dreamy basement? What is this place and who is she?

She is an ancestor of love and carries his losses when he cannot, when he can carry only his bones. She carries his soul too if he cannot, when for hidden reasons he must be blank like paper on a basement floor.

Those tunnels, I wonder, what are they to her? Fallen angels have no such eyes and the subway is not hell, I know this. Why does she live there?

This is bad. Flailing in his story, he conjures stale angels and devils. It is the underground, the sub city where grief flourishes and why not, for your losses run below more than anywhere else. He will know this, that loss is animate, beating sub surface, that this young beauty carries his losses where loss is best preserved. He will know soon.

Suppose I find her again on some dim station, how would I recover my things? Hold her by the eyes and shake her? Talk them out of her or steal them back? If the thief of soul can't die what do you do? Besides, what is one more empty vessel in a degraded world?

No more of this. Not talk, not theft. He will search for her, yes, but let us without delay speed his story to its end and halt the words of this clumsy narrating hero falling so carelessly through the heavy air. Michael, we'll call him, lost many women, carried pain, heard the haunting, howling wolves in his dreams, faced the mirrors and clocks after sunrise. Such was his life until one twisted morning a woman who seemed to be outside of time but was no doubt a creature of this warm world took his losses into her eyes which then became blacker and more beautiful and even more earthly. Relieved of pain, nightmares, and clocks, he was not empty, his soul gone. He complained, searched the subway for months, finally found her on a downtown station and demanded his things, which she sternly refused to surrender. Nothing would move her, not words, not the angry hands he placed on her eyes. This was the law to which he was subject and she would say no more. He walked the streets that seemed at every hour like early morning, saw only empty busses, empty bottles, pens without ink, stomachs without food, cars running on empty, the open hands of street people, heads without hats or brains, wrists with no ripple of pulse. Nothing could he see but the empty. Worse, the marching bones coiled in wires and waves that had so often sickened him, their mouths moving, their eyes fixed, mobbed the night streets more than ever. Nothing full, all vacant. At night when he slept he gripped the edges of his mattress in fear of levitating, so empty was he, and when after months of being hollow in a world where nothing appeared but the hollow he met someone. She was walking in the park, fully lit by the currents of her gadgets, stripped of everything but chatter yet with presence enough to call out. She had been looking for him, she said, waiting a long time yet certain that he would arrive. They walked for hours through the large park as she talked endlessly of her love. But Michael could not love her without his grief or his soul. In the enormous shadows cast by twilight he saw the history of Undead love, every creature of blood and cape that had ever been in the arms of a bat-winged lover. Those shadow stories multiplied by the second but there was no speed at which he could not absorb their narratives, and being himself so empty he could contain them all. Days passed, they met again, he still could not love her. Go home and sleep, she said. Later in dreams he saw her grieving over his loveless life, her tears falling freely through the wide-open spaces within her. Two days later he dreamed again and the Undead came once more and wept for him. Now he saw their tears too falling backward through their empty bodies, he saw their grieving bloodshot eyes that made the sun rise and share the secret that place, even Undead space, was but another word for soul, which after all had never been called a thing of substance. In the morning, empty man that he was, he returned to the empty woman, who was waiting in the park for his empty body. She had a gift for him: a small porcelain case containing her tears and the tears of the Undead, which at sundown he would pour into his hollow body before a wildly flickering candle and for the first time know the love of empty space, which no woman of the subway need ever help him discover again.

II.

Bastards, old and stupid, narcissism is the disease of our time, isn't it, and you infected, unable to leave this character on his own, making me tell my own story which a Nameless Lady never does because telling violates laws even we must answer to, nitwits, making me tell my story, making me tell, making me restore my character who is now twisted and bruised and battered story, making me intervene, making me begin it again with danger of everything collapsing as I fidget with a tale I gave to the world in the care of the Guardians, you as useful as the shit on the street, that I should have to set it right when you strip it off the tongue of the narrator whose tongue was doing just fine until proud and gutsy farts imposed their melodious tunes on a good story, sure I'm no master of metaphor and to think that I should have to ask you since when are Vampires pure except from the asses of phony lyricists chiming out dissonance and forgetting that the soulless of the earth trading themselves for microchips are never pure, that no storyteller at all should have to tell how on some subway stations, why the chichi 59th I don't know, she carried the history of his grief, he a young man who felt old with droopy eyes shadowed by long wavy hair to whom she couldn't tell him what he meant to her or explain the task of finding those whose pain she must carry, how she of the subway wandered station to station with his lost women heavy in her eyes and all who noticed felt drowsy before her beauty, how her heavy eyes slowed the trains now never on schedule and all women he stared at for more than five seconds wept in surprise under light rain while the men rode trains no more, how one night after much searching he found her on a downtown subway station minutes before the last train entered and not knowing what to do he talked endlessly on the empty platform hoping to relieve her of his losses, how he put his fingers on her eyes, shook her and shouted and threatened to kill her but nothing would give, how the station lights went out and he heard her soft voice and was suddenly in love but how she could not follow him to the street and therefore each night he met her below before the last train entered in order to be alone with her, how, you stupid bastards, they kissed on the empty platform and after one month she was gone so that at the bottom of the stairs was a note written in the composite hand of the women she carried, each letter differently formed that told how it was time for her to return to a place on this earth he would not understand, how she could not surrender his lost women but he would soon know why, how, I know I'm a clumsy repeater, he grieved and wept over the dark streets with that wrinkled letter flapping under light rain and a sky that would turn black at dawn at which time he would mourn another loss but once home he slept instantly and in his dream she took the sadness he felt for her into her own eyes knowing it was his deepest pain and would make her more powerful and how she now carried herself in her eyes, the strongest grief of all, along with his other losses and walked the underground distributing this grief to the empty, multiplying it, slowing the trains to a stop, even halting the clocks till at sunrise there was heavy rain and thunder and lightning streaked through the bedroom window and added its own architecture to the many shaped letters of the wrinkled note he clutched, still asleep, and how this letter was all that was left in place of his soul, a lousy plain piece of paper with writing, how his soul never returned but not for some son of a bitch grieving Vampire love, but because there are those who have to pay, those who must give what they have so that empty vessels will be filled and the smell removed from this earth, how those who pay will walk the streets with a special blankness all their own and recognize each other because this blankness is the space where was once stored precious possessions and as for you drooling clowns enchanted by the Undead who are not special but too dumb like you to know that they can't see their image in the mirror because they don't exist and if they did they'd stink the mirror to fragments just like that yellow teeth bum he sees in the morning, you'll never touch my stories again, no, I'll care for my own and tell what I sent out and with a little time and a little polish which I've never had for want of practice tell them well, because this earth needs stories of the empty but not tales touched by dunces who don't know the meaning of empty and can't keep their withered tongues off our characters who will if left alone move out of the words of our stories and into the world to find ways to fill things again and return to the earth what she's lost and restore to the spaces within the flesh the things that are missing. And his name isn't Michael.

Susan Rich

The Mapparium

Boston, Massachusetts

In geography class we learn the world
of oceans, continents, and poles. We race
our fingers over mountain ranges and touch
rivers lightly with felt tip markers. Deserts, islands,
and peninsulas tumble raw and awkward
off our tongues. *Kalahari, Sumatra, Arabia.*

We visit the Mapparium on a field trip.
A made-up word we learn
for the place where the world resides.
We clamor in with falling socks and high octave squeals
Palermo, Kabul, Shanghai,
exploring the globe, crossing its circumference we take flight —
touch down on the see-through bridge.

The world as it was, a time called 1932,
stays in a room — retracts our breath,
our lives — makes history into color and light.
We look up at the Baltic's, see *Lithuania, Latvia, Estonia,*
lands my grandmother left. Sixteen
and wanting the world.

I want to stay inside this world, memorize
the patterns of blue that reveal
the origins of every sea.

A wave hitting stone is the sound my voice leaves
as a pledge of return on the glass.
Feet to Antarctica, arms outstretched
like beacons towards Brazil—
I'll take this globe for my own.

Ruth Lepson

If You Speak

The title of the novel is unclear.
Even the very notion of the year's unravelling.
So, when time no longer exists
For us, who rush into the atmosphere,
The bells seem meaningless and
The earth shoots through ceaseless space
Into another galaxy, a strangest place.

So we were foolish to create a plan,
Excluding others not of our ilk.
All soft silk, all love unimportant,
Impotent and Greek, exclusive.

Don't say a word. If you speak
Speak silently to those we've
Destroyed, cavalierly.

Sassan Tabatabai

Sufi Haiku

by the time I spoke
a breeze rustled through the leaves
and you disappeared

★★★

like a drop of rain
that falls into the ocean
I dissolve in you

★★★

I rush upon you
as the moth rushed the flame
my sinews ablaze

★★★

plant me in the soil
water me with spit and tears
so that I may grow

★★★

what tongue does she speak
whispering words of comfort

to the outbound soul

★★★

breathe deep into me
the reed that's cut from its bed
so that I may sing

★★★

the blind earthen worm
overjoyed by the cool mud
knows nothing of silk

★★★

minaret leaning
under the weight of forced prayer
held up by the wind

★★★

by the river bank
I turned over every stone
trying to find you

Philip Nikolayev

The Poet Stopping by Some Brains Etc.
For Stephen Sturgeon

Whose brains these are I think I know,
Although I still have leagues to go
To apprehend in all this mess
The origin of consciousness.

It is a solitary funk
To watch the mind dispose of junk,
Tabula rasa it no more,
Containing food for thought in store.

My gentle mental daimon tugs
Upon gray matter or whatever:
A simple simile closely hugs
What to the lake is water.

So placid here the mind occurs,
Temporarily heals the nerves,
Achieves a unique balance,
A momentary wellness.

The wells of thought are drowning deep,
The sleep of reason gives me the creeps,
And all this nonsense on my lips
Ain't worth so much but cheers me heaps.
The wells of thought are drowning deep.

White Cranes

A village boy of 6, Ramakrishna
happened to be walking by some rice paddies
with a basket of puffed rice. Suddenly
a big dark cloud gathered.
Watching it overtake the sky, he saw
a wedge of white cranes streaking
below the blackness above.
So transfixed was he by the sight
that he physically passed out,
puffed rice flying
in every direction.

As a young man, I came
from very far north to Kamarpukur,
to those very rice paddies, or similar,
but there wasn't a cloud in the sky.

Not yet.

Raquel Balboni

holy rocks

i imagined pulling down the biggest pair of scissors id
    ever seen from a deep blue starry night
up from the sky some big hands dropped them into my
    smaller hands
i clung to them and felt the breathing of their sharp
    blade
they had a smell of either blood or love

around me in the inescapable claustrophobia of thinking
    too much, a guiding spirit spoke to me
it provided me with the tool to cut out of this plush
    kingdom
where i was a hard shelled tube full of organs blue and
    sinking

there was a promise to get out of there

to think about it less
to clean and declutter
to get around it

in the blinking ember of freedom
there was a standing pillar so thick and strong
it was the bone of soul

i bowed to it in a shaky collapse

i wept over the trouble it took to find it there,

some center.

nothing found outside
will be the fulfilling prophecy
for the universal hole
screaming

...

let myself be known of this suffering
yes, it is here inside, the feeling
but not the bulb, the bulb curled up inside itself

protected by a tomb so soft it was once disemboweled
by an army of black dogs with no teeth

let myself be known of this truth one way
orange faced smiling people shrug from the corner
the corner as big as a good luck stone
that is thrown at the side of my head

i am outside the grabbing hold of these unsteady hands
nothing seems different besides the location of service
where my brain waves lift like cobras
someone somewhere else decides

what to spread and what to conserve
the first birth rite is holding on
finger bones stiffen

the last birth rite is letting go
completely,

shattering

Fanny Howe

The Continuance

The structure failed to cohere at the end of the struggle.
It had some color but too much light.
That is, it could be located
Even if there were only scraps scrawled in blood and char
The bones she added to the mixture turned the paint
    life-brown.

There was violence, the victims could tell they were
    being failed.
Now the pile is housing. A plank to sleep on.
She had lost her chance and seemed forced from the
    dark burrow of her soul.
Her children cry:
Rebuild! Mash the leaves into glue and smear on green
    stones.

Too late. She has become a new form of life.
She doesn't care where she sleeps or continues after the
    war.
Who will take pity on this strange creation—the god of
    Nature?
Void of human cruelty. Empty of images.
Its intention clear.

Ben Mazer

Crane, Duncan, Schubert, Schwartz, the Thirties rest

in cinema notes, Ashbery-esque notations…
College of royal flowers, they were the best
at giving consciousness rotations…
Their outer-space ways hurried and condensed
the universe into a ciphering
love-giving flower of the cosmos sensed
and bent as in a mirror with love's sting…
Thus, they must crash and crack the face of fate
and crush the very gift that made them thrive,
the purposeless exactitude of hate;
thus cosmic seers have lost the will to live…
Yet live on, in city buildings up on high,
unless it be that all this life they die.

The Museum

At 11 a.m. the museum is still open,
and I arrive there later than myself,
but ready to catch up so quickly
that I recognize all the paintings
and denigrate the sonnets of Edwin Denby.
It doesn't matter, Andy Warhol or Picasso,
or if Wyndham Lewis should cease to exist.
They are all there among the flowering Mexicos,
and the frame of a car wreck is so New York,
you might go out and do anything, or be anyone.
Up here in Boston the mind is chilly
and swept by the fogs of the coming snow,
an older dowager who perpetuates Christmas
amid a sea of small dogs.
O, the seas are deep as any picture,
the pirate and the girl on the crumbling cliff,
the long sun leaning through the autumn leaves,
encyclopedias of cereal feeding Leon Errol
(I think of the junk trucks I have seen),
steep as any hill for a rabbit's burial,
the cat chasing fireflies under the cherry tree.
I cease to exist—I am maybe Joe Green,
wireless and coded in the manuals of Korea,
connected to me by the snow in The Dead.
But O, Mrs. Gardner, Mrs. Isabella Gardner,
is elevated to the estate of Europe,

frosty as a soldier. I long to get home…

The Last of the Contessa

Chapter One

When I was a very young man, I pulled a slim volume down from the shelves of my father's library. Its title must have intrigued me, or perhaps I had heard of it. I was all of eight, and the book was The Great Gatsby. As I began to read it, the strange, tortuous prose seemed as incomprehensible to me as a foreign language masquerading as English, and though I struggled with each word, each phrase, each sentence, accustomed as I was even at that age in my precociousness to dipping into such works in my father's library as those by Freud and Shakespeare, I could make out no meaning whatsoever in the peculiar language unlike any I had ever heard, which yet seemed to carry within it a veiled significance, which I could only suppose I would understand when I had grown a little older and reached maturity—a state which I imagined as so far off and removed from my present condition that I could hardly imagine it could ever exist at all. I have read that book a number of times since, at intervals in my life that have seemed like periods of catharsis, when the mind and soul needed to dip itself into some kind of familiarity to consolidate, ritualize, and confirm a sense of refreshment and renewal, and expunge itself of its notions, and though I have taken away from it an almost heartbreaking sense of the tragedy of life in all its exalted romanticism and stunned and stunted desire, it is not until this moment that I have understood what long ago should have been most obvious about the situation in its entirety.

That would be a very good place to end my first paragraph, and it would be a nice touch in any work of fiction to delay the revelation of my meaning to some later point in my narrative, revealing it only by increments, but the fact is that the plainness and simplicity of what has now struck me, and which may seem so trivial as to suggest or indicate no meaning or revelation at all, to those perhaps who have lived lives of action instead of the more sheltered life of philosophy and meditation, has given me not merely a starting place from which to unfurl all I have ever known or felt which has seemed to me like wisdom, without myself being wise, but has given that wisdom which is in life itself outside of us, a place from which to unfurl my own existence in the least canny way possible, by the statement of bare fact. For it is not merely that Gatsby was a bootlegger, and that when we are young and struggling we are shocked by the revelation of his own sordid and unimpressively trivial past, but the fact of what we should or might have realized all along that is significant: indeed anyone with some experience in the ways of the world could and perhaps would have realized all along that Gatsby was a bootlegger, without the book's author ever having told it to us, and that such triviality in his personal past as Gatsby chose so seemingly momentously to hide is really the stuff of any life of significance or impressive grandeur.

Although I came from the East, I lived for many years in California, in a small town which a friend of mine once described as possessing an atmosphere of "languid mysteriousness." It was a town that, like many California towns, in those residential areas with their small Spanish cottages dating from the 1920s, never seemed to reveal a tinge or trace of human life. No figures moved behind the blueish, mirrory darkness of their windowed interiors, and not a soul passed one in the stifling lament of their forlorn yet peaceful sidewalks. The cottages lay low to the ground, surrounded by the timeless, inert fury of wan greens and pale greens crisscrossing each other in a kind of symphonic silence of trees, and bushes, and lawns, and one felt that a kind of concealed divinity of religious iconry and old and forgotten objects must have lain beyond their exteriors in impregnable libraries and other stationary manifestations of lives long ago put on hold. At bookstores and at yard sales, which in our indigent youth we ever seemed to be stumbling upon like hidden pockets in dreams of eternity, an endless profusion and clutter of rare and delicious old books, records, and artifacts seemed to emerge as if from the ocean of time and the proximity of what once must have been the richness and grandeur of Hollywood. One could find anything there, but it didn't seem to matter beyond the personal joy it caused us, and the pronounced confirmation of our own sense of existing as particles in the spectacle of history, for there was no one there to barter or exchange ideas with, and the teeming life they must have represented was long gone as surely as if it had never existed.

The streets stretched out in pale blues which brought back to me violently a sense of the indefinable meaning of my own childhood in an Eastern town, when I would tag along endlessly after my mysterious, brilliant, and schizophrenic uncle Lou, whose own past and actual activities seemed as mysterious and unknowable to me as the enormities of his founts of brilliant, iconic chatter, a spider's web of implications and resonances, indications undefined, a mixture of chemistry, architecture, aesthetics, mathematics, practical invention, and the history of the Jews. As I always have, I wanted to know what I had missed, and I could only suppose that the world and time that had preceded me had existed in some other dimension which for me really bore no reality at all, except in that of the imagination, like the substance or meaning of the Beethoven or Mozart sonatas that Lou was always playing on the piano when he wasn't continuously pacing up and down the black and white checkered marble halls of my maternal grandfather's enormous self-built estate. Something about hanging around the community pool with him always made me feel a little restless. I called him "raisin-belly" because of an enormous mole on his stomach, and when we walked out on autumn days to where he would buy me thirty-five cent novels and comic books off the racks of the tiny corner drugstore, he would always spit on the church as we rounded the corner.

Now that I'm grown up a bit, and have lived in places like Southampton and Boston and New York, and have gone to three prestigious universities in the East, and in any ordinary sense found myself, all that seems to matter no less, but in fact to have hardened into a kind of substance of life itself, in any of its permutations. Thus it is that I begin to tell my story. Because I'm writing a book about the past not existing.

★★★

I received my degrees pretty early on in the game, after some earlier lapses that discouraged me so badly that I permitted myself to remain on the west coast for a number of years, living the proverbial life of the starving artist, if not quite that of the eternal scholar, and surprised myself to discover that enough wine and women, as well as the occasional more illicit vice, were enough to promote a semblance of what I took to be poetic inspiration, but which was probably that psychosis which is common to very young men with artistic ambitions, until the whole project wore so thin that I was forced to admit defeat. Back East, a chance encounter with Sir

Malcolm Ashingdon, the famous literary critic, to whom I was introduced by some mutual painter friends, was enough to get me into Harvard, where I was so happy to have any social standing whatsoever that I applied myself with enough diligence to attain an honors distinction, and became a sort of protege of the most distinguished faculty of the English Department, including the great Irish poet Sean Kavanaugh, who would take me walking around the Yard in my conspicuous candy-striper duds, and Chester Puddington who had been close friends with Lowell and Eliot, and who spent many hours with me in his rooms explaining the excellences of my poems to me. At Harvard, I fared a little better, though I easily fell into the somewhat obscure tradition of what the literary biographers refer to and really mean when they speak of an "outsider"—that is, one who finds that poetic ambition tends to put him at the very fringe of college life, and at odds with the university—and being somewhat older meant living off campus and having little access to the Clubs or to that glamorous and famous student social life which is where all the big-time careers and corresponding lifetime connections are really made. The outsider who is a Harvard poet tends to find himself at odds or even fully embattled with the stern sobriety of the college officials, who, as much as college officials can, live in the real world, and is often a casualty of his own defiance, artistic and intellectual snobbery, or a chronic inability to keep up with papers, classes, tutorials, exams, and what not, extending even to the social mores of college life and a complete comprehension of or assent to the fine print of college rules and regulations. Most either drop the university or are dropped by the university. Hearst himself, though his field was journalism, was a notorious and even the archetypal example, his Harvard career ending when he gave each of his professors a bronze chamber pot with the respective professor's face engraved at the bottom, and placed a live donkey in the President's office, with a sign hanging from its neck that read, "Now There's Two Of Us." Or so the story is told.

But I managed to hang on, and my grades weren't bad at all, and before long Sir Malcolm mysteriously materialized again, this time inviting me to pursue a graduate degree at the university-within-the-university that with his own brand of defiance he had started at another prestigious institute of scholarship and academic charades, giving me what at that point was the shock of my life in doing so, for my many years of indigence out west had acclimatized me to an inward sense of social inferiority, and a certainty that I would end my days in abject poverty or worse. Sir Malcolm was so brilliant that when he asked me to meet him on a bench in the middle of a large public park at dusk, and bring us two coffees, I thought I must be in some kind of dream, and his incredibly mystifying torrent of incomprehensible double-speak, all delivered in a British accent so sophisticated, elastic, and rapid that I could barely make out a word he was saying and could only dumbly nod "yes" at what seemed like significant intervals while the total blankness of my own comprehension crashed like a humming silence around my head, and I was convinced that Sir Malcolm must have lost his mind completely to be devoting two hours of his time in such a peculiar activity with, of all people, myself, and I did not understand a jot of what had happened. When I recounted what had transpired to a friend of mine who was a real graduate student at Harvard, he simply said, "He's inviting you to do a Ph.D. with him." "A Ph.D.?" I exclaimed, in total disbelief, sure that I had just witnessed the oncoming complete deterioration of Sir Malcolm's mind into explosions of nonsensical mania. "He's practically beating you over the head with it." And so it was that I began my graduate career.

My relationship with Sir Malcolm had been odd from the start, in that we initially met when my painter friend encouraged me to write him a letter, and enclose with it some of my poems, and I responded to this suggestion by recounting in my letter the story of how a certain famous professor of classical poetry, to whom I had similarly sent neophyte poems a number of years earlier, had responded after an interval of two years by having his secretary phone every relation of mine in the area with the seemingly urgent message that he wished to see me. He must have lost my message, or I must have become unreachable through several changes of address, and when I excitedly called his office, the secretary who I reached on the end of the line told me that Professor Marrowplex had passed away of a heart attack forty-five minutes earlier. No trace of what he wanted to see me about was ever discovered, and I related the story to Sir Malcolm with great relish, closing with the intimation that I hoped that Sir Malcolm himself would not die as a result of receiving a letter from me. I supposed that Sir Malcolm enjoyed this sort of brazen unfiltered effrontery from a young poet, and it was that which had done the trick, for he shortly afterwards invited me to lunch at his faculty dining club, sent several pages praising my poems in detail, and mysteriously remarked that we had a great deal in common.

Sir Malcolm was patient and tolerant and fatherly with me, but when after five years of living the high life on the enormous stipend I continuously and mysteriously received from the bursar's office, I had produced not a page of my dissertation, he hissed at me ominously one day as we passed each other in the department mail room, "Don't let me down." Shortly afterwards I was invited to lunch at an Indian restaurant a short walk from Sir Malcolm's enormous office, the largest of any professor at the university, and was told in so many words that Sir Malcolm had no belief whatsoever that I would finish my degree, and that I should do everyone a favor by dropping out immediately.

It was that night and the next that I spent the two darkest nights of that soul that I shall ever expect to experience in the whole of my lifetime, sinking to the utter bottom of human dejection as I drowned my desperation and visions of a catastrophically miserable end to my days in the only solace of indulgence I could think of that would afford me a chance to absorb and reflect on what had happened in my stunned, shocked stupor—I rented half a dozen talking pictures from the early '30s, which as luck would have it all turned out to be melodramas about victims of the depression who resorted to tragic suicide in the end, and watched them end to end. This instilled in me such most extreme, agonizing horror—an emotion so dark and horrible and low that I expect or hope never to experience it again—that I made up my mind then and there to begin writing my dissertation at any cost the very next day. And I did.

For the next nine months I virtually locked myself in my tiny apartment, the attic of a run-down historical house run by a little old Italian lady with more mood swings than a bipolar chimpanzee, churning out page after page as I sank deeper and deeper into what the experts call a "major depression" as the rigid monotony of my work—for it was a bit of technical textual analysis that required virtually nothing of the imagination—and my self-imposed total lack of social contact with even a single living soul, along with the complete restriction I had placed on myself of not engaging in the relief of any recreational or human activity of any kind. Finally, I broke down completely and lay for weeks in a fetal position on my bed in the dark, chain-smoking and flicking the ashes and an ever-increasing pile of butts into a giant cookie tin in the middle of the bed. It was the summer, and stiflingly hot up there, and my walls, if anyone had turned on a light to be able to see them, were dotted all over with the skeletons and corpses of various insects I had murdered but had not had the temerity or even the wherewithal to scrape from the walls, so that my room, except for the pile of empty and festering yoghurt cups, ice creams cups, cigarette packages, and frozen dinner trays that completely filled the corner of the room directly over the shoulder of my desk, resembled a cave filled with prehistoric fossils and the primitive carvings of cavemen, or perhaps the insect room of an anthropological museum. The screen of one window was completely torn out where I had cut it with a knife to get into my apartment when I had locked myself out one especially discombobulated night, and in the rude summer heat an occasional bat would fly in and circle madly around the room flapping its wings while I attempted in one motion to beat it away with a broom and duck in terror from its frantic oncoming passes at me.

That bat might have been a metaphor for my life at that time, and the worst of it came when I learned—of all places by reading it accidentally on the internet—that my best friend, an 81 year old poet in California named Hugo Marble, had blown his brains out with his World War II service revolver an hour earlier in Mill Valley. That stopped me up completely, and it was only after attending the ash scattering on Mt. Tamalpais and visiting the small central coast town where Marble had lived out his days, and seeing the little cottage from which so many of our all-night telephone conversations had been conducted on his end of the line, that I experienced so profound a catharsis as to set me back on the right track again so that I was able to enter the final stretch and finish my dissertation at the last possible moment and in the nick of time to pass my defense in April and graduate with my class. My dissertation, a critical edition of the works of an obscure nineteenth-century poet from New England, was immediately snapped up for publication by Harvard University Press, and for the first time in my life I felt a sense of vindication and of being on the right track. It was then that I disappeared to Manhattan for a while to fool around and while away a summer utterly unimpinged upon by books of any kind, enjoying encounters with girls in the park, and generally running wild. That was how I met the Contessa.

Chapter Two

The Contessa's funeral in Jamaica, Long Island, was an inconspicuously conspicuous affair. The head of the coffee federation was there, and the granddaughter of one of the famous cold war presidents. I stood off at a distance in my gray slicker in the rain, hatless and without an umbrella, paying my respects, like everyone there, to the life-size statue of the Contessa that contained her ashes. The Contessa's family stood ceremoniously to one side, looking for all the world as disparate a group of characters as the gang of thieves in The Maltese Falcon. Signor Bardini looked up and nodded at me with a look of recognition as if he were handing me a cigar, the sole instance of a break in character from their intent concentration on the muted grave.

The statue seemed as wrong as wrong could be, or maybe it was my mood, because I had to admit the gossamer whiteness, the wing-like folded arms, and the smiling unsmile of inequalable beauty contrasted perfectly with the triumphing uprightness of the world-leading arrow which slew her, held in her right hand. Being young, and at the height of her dawning powers, already having for an instant come to the notoriety of the world, she was perfect in death. There was no way she could possibly become undone.

Rain suited the Contessa better. Its insistent nowhereness of sound and discolor reminded me of her fidgeting hands in their white gloves, or naked, as in the evening when we could not decide between chess or a movie. It reminded me of what I thought her mind must be like, soft, and tepid, and gray, a comforting fog in which one did not have to see people one knew.

When it was over, I slipped off unnoticed and hailed a cab for Sardi's, where I drowned my already numb spirits in a succession of dry martinis, asking the waiter to leave the empty glasses, as I stared archetypically at their bottoms. On the way, I had managed to avoid two or three big Hollywood producers who I had known a little bit because of the Contessa. The last thing I wanted was to get caught up in anything that even faintly smacked of a business discussion. In fact, it was death that seemed to have put me in business.

My mind played over the relentless rush and frenzied layers of the past year, the time in which the Contessa and I had been inseparable.

My mind travelled back to the first day I had seen her.

I must have bumped into the Contessa a dozen times that day in Manhattan, starting shortly before noon in the subway station next door to the women's lingerie store on 34th and 8th.

She came in while I was eating dinner in the Cafe Reggio and ordered a cannoli and a cappuccino.

She took a photograph of me. Then she turned her attention to her cannoli.

We wound up sitting all night until dawn on the

18th floor open terrace of her mother's apartment on Central Park South—on the one side of us all of Central Park, beneath us toppling in our lawn chairs, above the enormous flashing lights signaling to all the world their catastrophic messages beneath the immense clock, and the temperature, lit up for all to see…

It was hot, and the Contessa sipped a beer slowly. We were drinking beers and smoking cigarettes and telling each other our life stories. The hues from the lights overhead kept changing from yellow, to pink, to green…

One night in a Starbuck's in the west 60s I was raving about how the people who had been hired by the military to make a study of faces were wrong in thinking that they could identify or interpret all possible facial expressions. A British fellow a bit younger than me leapt up to his feet and declaimed what I was saying, insisting that what I was saying was very foolish. There was something sad in him, and we tried to be amiable. He converged with us on the sidewalk and we smoked cigarettes in the Night Air. He asked me if I knew Sean Kavanaugh, which was odd, because I did. I described how Kavanaugh had plagiarized my early poems. He described drunken debauches with the sons of Ezra Pound and Robert Lowell. It all seemed so odd. We asked him if he was a spy. He told us his father had been in British military intelligence, in Persia, but that he had never wanted that life for himself. He was a scholar of classics. He gave us his phone number and sauntered off to get some sleep.

★★★

It was shortly before I was to meet the Contessa's family, that first crazy summer, that I received the news from Italy that my parents' rented Italian roadster had gone off a high cliff into the Mediterranean outside of Naples, leaving me, much to my puzzled surprise and astonishment, for I had no way of explaining this, and no idea where the money had come from, an immensely wealthy man.

The Contessa and I rented a roadster of our own, utterly oblivious to the symbolism or the irony, and headed straight for her family's house in Southampton, arriving at nightfall, after everyone had eaten their summer dinner, and an unidentified cast of characters, introduced rapidly if at all, was breaking up for the night, though some of the men remained gathered 'round the summer table sipping their brandies and smoking their cigars.

In the morning we hurriedly bought me an array of evening suits, shirts, socks, and ties, a pair of sunglasses with an air of wealth to hide the fact that I had been weeping, and a new pair of expensive English shoes. This, the Contessa explained to me, was so that her mother would be suitably appeased by my appearance, and so that anything awkward in my comportment or demeanor or any general ineptitude would be sufficiently disguised for the occasion. I was to watch and listen, but also to fit in. As it happened, this came quite naturally and easily, and the family embraced me quite readily as what they had decided was an intellectual and a writer, and I was treated to the tough, witty, knowing, backyard repartee about hotels, commodities, distribution, mortality rates, government roads, air routes, mineral deposits, populations, cultural differences, the high spots just then in New York, and taxes, as if I were an acknowledged man of affairs.

The Contessa told her mother that I had recently suffered from a mental breakdown, and in the morning, while she went off with her mother in search of improperly evaluated treasure at thrift shops and yard sales, I sat for the first time in the light of day in the immense backyard with the pool and the Asian garden, sipping black coffee from a china cup, and taking in the surroundings. For the first time in the ten years or so that I'd been running, I felt at peace, if a little shattered and aimless. After all, I was now a wealthy man, and could afford to do nothing but concentrate on my internal well-being. But this illusion, too, was quickly shattered. Cousin Nicholo quickly found and took the seat next to mine at the white summer table, and lit the remnants of yesternight's somewhat battle-weary cigar. "How do you like it here?" he offered straightforwardly, with the air of a man who is never afraid to admit a newcomer to the family.

"It's lovely. I've needed a break for so long, and we both wanted to get away. It is very good to meet the family."

"You'll like it here. Everyone can see right away that you make the Contessa very happy. She has led a hard life. You've saved her."

I was later to learn that Nicholo was the back sheep of the family. He owed money to all of his cousins, with the exception of the Contessa, and also to Signor Bardini (perhaps the principal).

In the evening, cousin Giacomo arrived from Khali with his wife, children, and two rather stunning female secretaries. He owned hotels in all the big cities in Colombia, owned all of the rice fields in Colombia, had sold all of the milk in Colombia to a Dutch company, and had a business chartering unused airplanes in the middle of the night for private purposes from the national airline, which had been sold to one of the Fortune 50 for a song by the Contessa's family, who had started it shortly after world war one, before Juan Trippe got his hands on it for a time by secret arrangement in the 1930s, and it was now a 2 billion dollar business. Giacomo was inscrutably boyish in his t-shirt, sports sneakers, and tossed back haircut, and disappeared after a day or so, leaving the wife, children, and secretaries behind, as he went off on an unspecified yachting trip off the coast of Long Island that seemed to require a great deal of luggage.

That night we walked down the street with high, trim hedges past the Vanderbilt estate, and onto the white sand under what seemed like a billion blazing stars. I have honestly never seen so many stars, anywhere I've been. We lay on our backs, and listened to the surf, and watched dozens of shooting stars flit by, one after another, as if it were a show for us alone. The Contessa said, "I don't know what I shall make of myself in this life. Do you know what you shall make of yourself in this life?"

"Listen, Contessa. If I knew what I was doing I'd already be doing it. Why doesn't your family give me a nice lush job managing one of their hotels or airplanes?"

"But you are already working for the family."

"Me working for the family? What do you mean?"

Then she showed me the general staff listings for all their hotels in Colombia. I was listed as General Manager for each one…

What did I have to do with The Great Gatsby? I didn't have as many shirts as he did, but the ones I had were all first rate, and worth weeping over. Because it's what's inside the shirt that women weep for.

To love a woman that badly, that she is the world. It is the rarest and most beautiful of emotions, of modes of perception, and it is certainly how I felt about the Contessa. That was evident from the instant we were off and running, telling each other everything we knew, everything we had ever been through… The

Contessa's troubles with her parents were of monumental proportions, and had brought her to the doors of death on at least one instance... She had even been kidnapped by her mother and held captive for two years in a nunnery in Santa Marta.

Gatsby might have been a producer in Hollywood, and could have been. There, too, our temperaments were like. But I was of the rentier class, though surrounded by great wealth, and captains of industry and state, and began to feel that my work was to absorb with my eyes and my ears, and my line of talk, all that was going on around me, with the idea of accumulating an ability to play a role and have moments of expertise. But I was marked out for failure from the start, not having been born into all that, and only through the Contessa's influence attain to standing while the activities of the house were beyond me, and never more than suggestive of a mysterious and puzzling world of comprehension and facility quite unknowable to me. I knew it was time to set out on my own.

Kit Janssen was my secretary. I can't exactly say what a secretary for someone like me actually does; most of the times in the morning I can't even remember. But I have a huge correspondence, and Kit helped me to keep all the half-eats and quarter-wits at arm's length. She was also a crack at research, any kind of research. Kit was tall and gangly and bony, but very feminine beneath a boyish, no-nonsense, ever-ready-to-do-battle sort of charm. She had long legs and a slim figure, and dressed impeccably in tailored suits and modest, attractive summer dresses. She was my sounding board for ideas, and always kept me on the right track; her voice was like the sound of my own mind churning away in all its obliviousness, accustomed as I was to feeding my cockiness with a seemingly endless run of correct decisions and satisfying small triumphs.

Next thing I knew I was approached by a very wealthy man in London who wanted to pour a lot of money into a magazine that I would edit. How he had heard of me, or why he wanted to do this, I couldn't make out, but I liked the odds, so I took the assignment. One night we were talking on the phone late…

"Why are you doing this?" I asked. "Are you in intelligence work?"

"I've heard of you and checked you out. You have talent and I want to support that. I've been wanting to run a little magazine of my own, and you're just the sort of man I've been looking for to edit it. No, I'm not in intelligence work. My parents were, in India, for the British. But I could never do that; I'm prone to paranoia and I'd be too scared."

Another one too scared for the Great Game. I mulled it over. I couldn't see what I had to lose.

Funny thing was, here we were—a couple of nobodies—and suddenly everyone in New York wanted to write for us. Almost the entire writing staff of one of the most famous conservative New York magazines dropped their piddling paychecks and rolled up their sleeves for us, as if they relished to cut loose and write whatever they wanted to write for a change. In no time, we were wreaking havoc all over town, and had established ourselves as a major threat in the New York publishing world. Even the top film critic for one of the biggest New York magazines was now writing exclusively for us… Our success seemed incomprehensible, almost a miracle… But it was a gentleman's sport…

We all went out to Sardi's one night to celebrate. My London sponsor, Kit, the Contessa, and myself. For some reason the headwaiter seemed to know us and we were delivered to one of the nicest and most conspicuous tables, where the headwaiter removed a great plaque that read "RESERVED" and sat us, telling us he'd have a waiter right over.

It was autumn now and practically the time when ice skating begins to take place all over the city. The cold winds shrink down the senses to their modal cores, and one sets store by a crumb of compassion to get one through the long winter. I had the Contessa, ravishing in her crown and jewels. Outside the streets zig-zagged like the streets of my youth in a small town connected to Boston, and I thought of how the elementary emotions were played on by this, as any musical figure, arpeggio, or scale.

Things were getting a bit hot with Kit, in that she had

stumbled her way into a job as the aviation columnist for The Washington Post, 30-lines which appeared weekly under the heading "The Logic of the Air." This meant frequent trips to Georgetown, and an ever-widening circle of strangers inquiring mysteriously about The Critical Review. Word seemed to have gotten out…

As to the Contessa, she was not exactly losing any time either. Because of her old Greenwich Village artist connections, a chance encounter with Robert De Niro left him more than a little impressed. Two days later, the phone rang from Hollywood, and the Contessa was being asked to come out for a screen test. I went with her, and we rented Irving Thalberg's old villa for the occasion, a white and yellow affair of one-and-a-half stories, with semi-external gardens, and of course, a large pool. We didn't even have anyone over. We just rented it, tossed our heads back, and laughed. The Contessa gleamed with vitality and life. I studied her, a private study of what would soon be an international phenomenon. For the Contessa, it could be said, was truly bigger than life itself. And that was the problem.

Wyatt Bonikowski

The Spider Sewed a Dream

His mother lay in the hospital bed, shrouded in spider's silk, breathing long sighs. His father pressed a hand on his back. Go on now, hug your mother. But the boy was afraid and would not touch her. A spider with a human face crouched in the high corner of the hospital room. Whose face was it? Not his father's, who hunched at her bedside and scratched his patchy beard, but some leering other. The spider sewed a dream for him with its needle-thin legs and offered it as a gift. I don't want your dream, the boy said. Years later he told his father how he dreamed his mother and the spider with the human face, and his father said something about the devil, the devil always on his tongue, and the boy thought, My father doesn't know how to read spiders' silk. I want your dream now, he told the spider, but by then the world had changed and there was no more spider, no more mother.

Soft Drink

The father placed the coin in the boy's palm, a reward for bravery because he had sat still in the barber's chair when the old man's hands shook and the clippers nicked his ear. The old man wiped the blood with a white towel. The boy dropped the coin in the narrow refrigerator and pulled the cold glass bottle out by the neck. Then his father took him to the movies where strangers rubbed the fuzz of his clipped head for luck. He wouldn't go through the double doors because he heard screaming on the other side. It's not real, his father said. It's made up. Other people went through and a white glow poured out of the doors and the screaming grew louder and the knocking and banging, too. Everyone wants to see it, his father said. It's fun. But then a boy passed by and whispered, No, it's real. They're killing people inside. His throat felt dry and he dreamed of slipping inside the narrow refrigerator, but his father dragged him down a long hallway and through a parking lot and into street after empty street until it began to rain, and his father all the time saying, Didn't we have fun tonight, didn't we have fun. The boy opened his mouth and drank the rain. The rain sang to him, Hush, hush now.

Yes, I Carried You, Said the Silver Light

The boy sat with his back against the door of his father's room and listened to his father's pen scratching on paper. I have my work, his father had said. Do you understand? It means something has taken over. It means I have to follow it. The boy listened to the pen and his father's faint whisper until he fell asleep against the door, and when he woke in the dark he found himself in his own bed and his father was screaming at the other end of the house. He stumbled through the dark until he reached his father's room. Did you carry me to my bed? he asked. His father's screams spilled from under the door in a pool of silver light. Yes, I carried you, said the silver light. The boy cupped his hands at the base of the door as if he could catch the light and lift it to his mouth. In the morning, his father knelt by his bed. I didn't mean to wake you last night, he said. I was writing and I lost track of time. The boy was relieved. That was all it was, writing.

A Wreckage

He was in the house where his mother had died, where he and his father now lived with strangers. The house was no longer theirs, his mother was a ghost, and he shared a room with the children he called brothers. One of them pressed his wrists into the hard mattress and dangled a rope of spit above his face, then sucked it back up, the brothers laughing, a joke, they said, a game. Let's play another game, the fathers said. The fathers lined them up against the wall in perfect silence. The dog's eyes widened, its snout held closed by a man's strong fist, dripping nose, a long slow whine from somewhere inside. The dog had a name—what was it? The boys called a name. A man shouted a name in his ear. He heard it often as he sank into darkness just before sleep, a shout calling him back to a shattered heart and pearls of sweat on his face and arms. He paced the room until dawn, then showered and dressed and stood in the sunlight from the window, which shined back at him like a mirror. Slowly, he told himself, he was climbing out of the wreckage.

Meagan Masterman

The LaFourchette Girl

At the top of Horseman's Hill stood a stately farmhouse. A kind and respectable elderly lady lived there in a house decorated by china teacups and other fineries rare in the countryside. She was well loved. One Sunday, the house burned in an inferno. The licks of heat could be felt from across the street. Not even the foundation remained. All the china was pulverized to shards. My whole family (mom, sister, me) watched. We stood across the street in the pitted dirt driveway of the LaFourchettes. That was the day I first spoke to Mandy.

The LaFourchettes lived in a trailer. There were seven of them: Mandy, her four sisters, their mother, and their father. They were religious. Their clothes were all homespun. The girls were homeschooled, which meant they knew nothing and could barely read. The eldest daughter was twenty-two with no inclination to leave home. The youngest was eight. All the girls were fat and docile, except Mandy. Mandy was rail thin and anxious.

I was thirteen, old enough in my parents' eyes to be gone from dawn to dusk. Mandy was fifteen, which in the LaFourchette household meant she wasn't old enough for anything.

I had seen Mandy often before I met her. Sometimes she'd be outside when I biked down her road. Sometimes she would bounce a ball in the dusty driveway. Mostly she watched. She watched the younger girls play or she watched the clouds take on shapes. She watched the spokes on my bicycle. She watched me.

On the day of the fire Mandy stood apart from the crowd, eyes glued to the flames. I walked over and stood six feet away from her. She moved back until there were eleven feet between us. A fire truck rolled up the hill, the siren so loud we both crammed fingers in our ears. When the blaring stopped she moved two feet closer. And that's how I knew we were friends.

I saw her again at the Planting Time Supper. Everyone in town came. We ate each other's casseroles and raised a pinch of money for the volunteer fire department. The LaFourchettes sat at the far end of the gym. They took up an entire table – Mr. LaFourchette at the head and Mrs. LaFourchette at the other end. The girls ate quickly and quietly, diligently working through mounds of tater tot hot dish and tuna wiggle.

I saw Mandy get up. I followed her through the metal fire door into the stairwell then off to the less-busy bathroom on the second floor. She retreated into a stall and I called to her. "You're Mandy, right?" I said as if I did not know, leaning against the white tile of the bathroom.

She nodded, watching me.

"I'm Cassie. Tomorrow I'm going down to the dam. You should join me. We can hang out. Be there at 4:00."

"Why?" asked Mandy.

"Why not? It'll be fun."

She looked at her shoes.

"There's nothing wrong with it," I said.

Still half in the stall, she waited a while before whispering "I'll try."

The next day I set my bike on the soft shoulder of the road, stuffing a flat chunk of mica under the kickstand so it wouldn't sink into the sand. I went to the creek that ran behind her trailer and waited. We stood on opposite banks. I asked her what her favorite thing was. She told me horses. I felt the same.

We spent lots of time together through spring and summer. We had grown quite close by fall and stayed out long after our teeth started chattering from the cold, stubbornly clinging to our diversions, mud caked on our shoes. I often told her what she must do with her life. It was much like I was planning to do. I told her she could rent a room from me in Boston once I got settled there.

I invited her to hang out at my house when my parents were gone. She was wary. It was one thing to be outside in neutral territory, another to enter the house of a non-believer like myself. But she came.

I put on American Beauty. I thought it would blow her mind. She watched it in effusive silence, the engaged-but-passive way I figured she took in sermons. At the end, I asked her what she thought. She balled up her fists and bit her bottom lip. "That man was lusting after a young girl. He should be ashamed. Forcing his lusts on her because why? Because he doesn't like his job?"

I scoffed. "You don't get it, Mandy."

"I don't want to get it."

We didn't speak for almost a month until I caught her once again bouncing a ball in her pitted driveway. I told her I wanted to buy her an ice cream. It was pumpkin ice cream season. The Dairy Joy would be closed for the winter in less than two weeks. She was reluctant as there was a special all-day church meeting the next day and she'd been looking forward to it. I convinced her to fake sick and made her promise to meet me right after her family left.

The next day she bounded out of the house, so pale she might really have been sick. She wandered around in a circle, clutching the stitch in her side and muttering "I did it."

She was a mess. Her distress ran up and down my arms like shivers. It took us an hour to walk to the Dairy Joy, me pushing my bicycle and asking her if she was still sure she didn't want to ride on my pegs. It was unseasonably hot and we were thirsty from walking.

"What do I get?" she asked me.

"Whatever you want."

"But I don't know what I want."

I snickered. "You do eat ice cream, don't you?"

She looked sheepish. "Sometimes."

"Then just get what I get. I always get a hot fudge sundae with rainbow jimmies. Because it's fall, I'll get it with pumpkin ice cream instead of vanilla." We sat out back of the Dairy Joy on a picnic table with peeling paint and discolored spots from sunbaked spills of ice cream. Next door was a Baptist church.

"Momma told me Baptists go to hell," said Mandy. "Do you think that's true?"

I shrugged. "Could be. I dunno."

She picked at the ice cream, shaving off from the side of the sundae rather than digging in.

"If you keep eating it slow you're gonna end up having to drink it," I said.

"I'm sorry," she said, but she let it melt anyway.

We went to dump our Styrofoam dishes into the sticky trashcan. "My stomach hurts," she said.

"Didn't you eat breakfast?"

"I couldn't. They would know I was faking."

A man came over, one hand in his pocket, the other with its thumb hooked into a belt loop. "What are you two ladies doing out here?" he said.

Mandy scurried behind the garbage can. "Leave us alone!" she said.

He moved closer.

I glared at him even though my knees were clacking. I grabbed Mandy by the elbow and dragged her out from behind the garbage can. "Come on, Mandy. I don't want to stay around creeps no more." The man shrugged and walked away.

"Why did you say my name? He's going to find me! He's going to show up at my house and Momma will know that I faked sick and I've been out here doing stuff with you that I shouldn't be doing."

"Cut it out. It's nothing. Just climb on my pegs."

"I'm going to die," she moaned, her hands pressed hard against her face. "I'm going to get killed in my bed and Daddy won't even be sad because he'll know I was a liar. What if he thinks that man was my boyfriend?'

"This is just the sugar talking. You're lightheaded and it's making you like this."

She glared. "You stop it! You tell me you're different but you're not. You order me around just like Momma and Daddy. You knew I didn't want to come out here but you made me do it anyway. At least they're doing it because they think it'll save my soul. You're doing it for no good reason! Do you think it's funny to get me so upset?"

She doubled up, clutching her stomach. The man watched us from across the parking lot, leaning on his truck.

"I'm sick. I lied about getting sick and now I'm sick. It's retribution."

"Get on the pegs. I'll get you home," I said softly. "Men are just creeps sometimes. But they won't do nothing, not here at the Dairy Joy. He won't remember you tomorrow."

I froze and looked at Mandy. In the middle of her hyperventilation, I noticed for the first time a pale sheen of a scar along her jawline. All these hours together and

I never saw. "What do you think about your parents?" I asked.

Mandy crossed her arms like a mummy. "Shut up. There's no time to talk anymore." And we didn't talk the whole way back, not even when we were at the foot of Horseman's Hill and my tired arms shook as they tried to push the bike along.

She hopped over the creek and headed for the trailer without a word, without a look. And that's how I knew we weren't friends.

I got older. I moved away from my hometown to Boston, with its skyscrapers and women clutching designer bags. I started coming home only twice per year, once for Thanksgiving and once in the summer to spend a long weekend. Sometimes I haul out my old bicycle from the shed and go for rides.

Some other family lives in the trailer now. I do not know them. I cannot ask them what happened to Mandy. Although it is a small town, it is New England. People do not pry, including myself.

But as I cycle around the countryside I think of her. And at the Dairy Joy I never order a hot fudge sundae with rainbow jimmies, no matter how much I want one.

Maria Pinto

CAMPING

Why had it taken me so long to notice that the tablet was not there? The spotless square of desk where it should have been was suddenly obvious, and mocking as an out-stuck tongue. *Just think of all the calamities that have probably befallen your son since you last paid attention*, the absence said, *and be nauseated*.

David never moved his tablet. Ever. He treated it as if the thing were riveted to the spot, and got grumpy when his visiting cousins attempted to abscond with it to other parts of the house. He took more pride in that Hanukkah present, given to him in lieu of the smartphone he'd requested, than any of his other possessions.

After school and an hour and half with his tutor, my boy usually sat at his desk, hunched over the screen for another half hour, roving Snapchat or Instagram and playing the odd pre-homework game. This time was his father's only concession to the way every other child seemed to live. Thirty minutes spent on something that wasn't a religious exercise and had nothing to do with school, officially anyway. Having negotiated this period of "play," I felt every bit the politician's wife.

But as I landed heavily on David's bed, the duvet smooth over sheets that lay in a chaotic tangle just below, the sight of the empty spot where the iPad should have been filled me with relief and dread in equal measure. I heard myself grunt, my throat too swollen to get a sob out. I'd been screaming most of the afternoon, sprinting from street to alley through the square, calling out David's name with all the lungpower I had, as if the whole city was a supermarket and David was still a misplaceable four-year-old boy. At any moment his little moon face could appear down one of the aisles and he would smile around his thumb and I would scoop him up and squeeze the air from his lungs. But David is 5'10" now, with his father's large frame. I can no longer contain him in those old bear hugs, and to strange eyes he's nearing manhood.

Even from inside the house I could practically hear them; all the neighbors' whispers have picked up, like a wind that bears up trash. What did they see before today through our un-shuttered windows? Did they think this moment was inevitable? If they had come to me with their concerns about our boy, ("He's so quiet!" "He never makes eye contact!") would I have listened?

Now they would mobilize. Articles would be published, "missing child" signs would be posted, social media pleas would be made, and police departments around the country would be alerted that someone important had vanished. The Jewish Community Center would deploy hundreds of volunteers to look for him.

But the missing iPad meant it was unlikely he'd been abducted by his father's political enemies, or that he was smuggled by human traffickers from the café where he was last seen, or that he was struck down and left for dead on a back road by joy-riders. Joel's mother, her voice elemental over the speakerphone in the next room, had just suggested this last horror. Here was a woman who still lived in a simple world that was crumbling from lack of conservation—anything bad that happened originated *outside* the homes of decent people. Later, though he'll remain taciturn with his therapist, David will favor me with this detail about his "time away": on the bus out of town, he programmed his iPad to alert him every time his name appeared in the news so that he could follow his own story. This was not the behavior of a child from the world my mother-in-law was versed in. But I remember that era she thinks we still live in now, and the day *I* ran away in it.

I was born to Russian immigrant parents, closely sandwiched between two very lively boys, and introverted myself, which is to say I was doomed to be ignored. When bringing home perfect marks failed to get my parents' attention, I turned to the rebellions that young girls will, like stealing trinkets from the drugstore, and applying a forbidden cosmetic face on the bus on the way to elementary school. None of this mattered since I never got caught. Bad girl behavior notwithstanding, I could no longer accept the gulag-like situation at home, namely the fact that my brothers went out to play while I had Saturday morning chores to do. It made me crazy to think that as I scrubbed away at the sink with Bon Ami, they were out on their bikes, gathering more of their infuriating inside jokes. So I took my case to the authority. I can still remember my mother's gentle admonition when I dared to confront her about the injustice: "Lazy boys have wives when they grow up, but who do lazy wives have?" The idea that I should brace myself for a life spent wandering from bathroom to bathroom with a toilet brush in my dishpan hands while my brothers got to revel in the fun parts of being grown-up was too much. It was time to run away.

I left early on a Saturday morning, looking back only to admire the fresh coat of blue paint my papa had favored our ranch-style home with the week before (I couldn't help it—I'd never seen the house in that light), and headed, through the brisk pink dawn, for the woods abutting my neighborhood. Our family had never gone camping (though I longed to), and I reasoned that I could learn to camp by doing it. Cartoon runaways took their provisions with them in luggage improvised from a large handkerchief and a stick flung over the shoulder; I had a couple of frozen TV dinners in a pillowcase tied with hair ribbon to the end of a broken umbrella. I could start a fire to heat the food, of course. I would hunt and forage when those supplies ran out. Thinking of those woods now, it's absurd I thought it possible to hide for very long in them.

Anyone who happened to be looking out of their window as I marched toward the end of our cul-de-sac would have had a good belly-laugh at the picture I must have made: *She has a sleeping bag, where does she think she's going? Don't let me forget to call Lillya when the hour is decent so she doesn't worry.* My mother would later tell me she got no less than five telephone calls from neighbors, and suggested that if I wanted to really make a go at stealth fleeing in the future, I should consider leaving before dawn, while *everyone* slept.

I spent the morning crunching through the brown and orange leaves, in that thrall every spiteful child falls under when they imagine a parent's contrition. First my mother would discover my empty bed, then she would fall to the floor weeping, and my father would join her there, *what terrible parents we are* tumbling from his lips. Then they would get my brothers to help search the property and Dima and Sasha would both despair, remembering all the times they ganged up on me to forward their inscrutable boyish ends. I imagined them arguing about who was most to blame for this unfortunate turn of events, and of course the answer would be Dima, and I hoped he would know this deep in his heart and resolve to bear that guilty knowledge for the rest of his life. I was still upset that, at Dima's suggestion, they'd spent the preceding Columbus Day weekend pretending that I'd died and that they couldn't hear me when I spoke.

"Dima, Sasha, I'm right here! Stop ignoring me," I was in tears.

"Ever get the feeling you're being watched or yelled at by something that doesn't exist?" Dima asked Sasha.

"Do you hear something? Is it the wind, maybe?" Sasha played along.

And then, when all hope of finding me was lost, say, a week or two from my great escape, I would reappear as a woman of the world, with a new trade, perhaps, and the knowing eyes of one who has seen enough in her days of wandering to be treated with respect.

Maybe his sophistication is what David wanted to illustrate to us with his four days away. At the hour of his return, when I am done with my hysteria, I will ask him if he planned to come back after his impromptu *rumspringa*. What would have happened if the police hadn't spotted him 200 miles away in New York City, kippah still dutifully affixed to his head even though the fear of heaven was apparently gone from him, taking pictures with a disposable camera as if he were a rightful tourist in Times Square? What would he have done if his saved-up allowance ran out and his parents had given him up for dead? Of course, by then, news of our search efforts would have rushed into his tablet every time he'd connected to WiFi, so I already had my answer: Yeah, right, Mom.

His only acknowledgement of my questions will be David's famous shrug-of-the-shoulders, and a polite request that I sentence him to whatever punishment was coming, already, so that he could get started on homework due the next day. Well, you can't pour water into a cup that's already full. So all I could do was tell him the story of my brief sojourn from family life and leave the punishment to his father.

If I'd perhaps been a more curious child that day in the woods, it might have taken me longer to get so bored that I started counting trees and hurling sticks at various fixed targets, like knotholes in tree trunks and low-hanging pinecones. I'd been in so much of a hurry to get out of the house without waking anyone, I'd neglected to pack *On the Banks of Plum Creek*, which I was halfway through reading. Since I'd already exhausted most of my homecoming scenarios, all of which ended in my consumption of large quantities of forbidden McDonald's fries, I'd begun to worry that the characters in *On the Banks* were carrying on without me. So it was with unequivocal relief that I noted the first fat drops of rain to make it through the canopy above.

"Well," I'd said to myself, "this adventure has been cut short by fate. Mother nature made it pour before I could get my shelter built."

As I ran out of the woods, so impatient to get back that I left my luggage behind, I tripped on a rock and landed wrong, according to my ankle. The air left my lungs and I felt the sting of pending tears in my sinuses. When I picked myself up and brushed off the leaves sticking to my clothes, I looked down to see a suddenly vocal baby mourning dove on the ground at my feet. Where was this poor thing's mother? The thatch of its nest had come undone from the fall, but I did my best to scoop the loose sticks up around the tiny, protesting bird and limped home, my ankle throbbing.

The smell of my mother's Zharkoye stew greeted me just inside the unlocked door of my house. I could count on tasting its deliciousness every Saturday at suppertime, a fact I only appreciated in that moment. The whole family was sitting in front of the television, watching an infomercial, and they seemed eerily complete without me. Like a well-cropped photo. My father had his arm stretched out along the back of the couch and my mother's hand rested on his hairy forearm. My older brother drove a matchbox car absently along the length of his thigh. My younger brother's mop of curly red hair was crushed against the side of my mother's breast, and his thumb was in his mouth, which one of my parents would correct in short order. Before I could say "Sasha's sucking his thumb," renewed chirping brought four sets of eyes to the spot where I stood, and I limped into the living room, cradling the tiny bird's tufty head in my palm. My mother let me see a plaintive smile as she got up. She brushed the wet bangs from my face as the psychic on television assured all potential patrons they would be satisfied with the results of their reading.

"Did you hurt yourself playing, my little doll? You're limping," Mother cooed. "And who is this? Who did you find?"

"I found her on the ground in the woods! Her mother just left her there!" I said between sniffles.

"What kind of a mother does that? Come, let's take our new friend to the kitchen and we'll put ice on that ankle." My father, Sasha and Dima crowded around as my mother alternated looking after my ankle and fussing over the little bird, which we gave water with an eyedropper. Sasha suggested that the baby was probably hungry, too, and that last night's leftover spaghetti was the closest thing we had to worms. My father said that this, my first sprain, was just my young body's way of letting me know to be a little gentler with it. At that moment, I was under the impression that my family hadn't even noticed I'd gone. But it mattered less to me than I might have thought. The image of them on the couch, utterly unperturbed by my absence, watching something inane on television, made me want to belong somewhere forever. Now, as I watch David skulk about the house, his newly liberated tablet casting an underhand light on his face while he checks his tickers and feeds, I doubt I could give him such an image of our life going on without him even if I wanted to, even if I tried.

End

Jenny Grassl

I SELL VESSELS OFF THE SHELF

you know I mean dishes   but there are ships

this store in its box   I blink in alloyed
incandescence   light of mercury

and tin   toxic like old news   yellowing
to taste   I yaw   from aisles of plates

to bowls   wish for an archipelago   cups
open their china mouths to take

a cache of alive   what's small and at risk
capillary   seaweed   root

what I keep   then lose   saying *thank you*
and *goodbye*   fingers leave

their grease   whorled onto inked webs
of dollars   fingerprints tell my genuine

from money and its spiders   giving change
you would think it was a final

giving up   I sip   I sup   but here is work
not done   for love   outside

a streak of street breaks   light run over by a car
splashed with last night's rain

my clerk reverie wakes to its darkery   town
sow slop and sue   sea run brown

with an alewife brook   the city burbles out
from this slough   to shine

enameled   street signs refigure   turn oracle
bejeweled   sung   in clear voice of marsh bird

Peter Brown

The Pillowcase

Between the ages of fourteen and sixteen, I sold a little weed. I got paid cash to pump gas at an Exxon station on the weekends. I worked for a dentist, too, Dr. Walsh and his beautiful wife Monica, who lived north of Waltham, a twenty minute bike ride away. They had ten acres of woods and twenty acres in pastureland. They had a horse, a pair of heifers they raised for beef, a family of pigs, and an overpopulation of cats.

Dr. Walsh drove up the lane one evening in his red Jaguar while I was pushing a wheelbarrow of manure out of the barn. He stopped, rolled down his window and told me to wait. He drove to the house and ran in and came right out with a plastic bucket. He drove back, got out of the Jaguar and set down the bucket with a pillowcase and a brick inside it.

"Inside the barn," he said, "is a bale of straw next to the door and under it a nest of new kittens. Did you see them? You tie them up in this pillowcase and put them in the bucket."

He pointed at the hose. "Then cover them with water. If they float, use the brick. Give them ten minutes. Then dig a hole by the compost and bury them."

"What do I do with the pillowcase?" I said.

"Just give it to Monica," he said, and squinted back at the house. "Or leave it on the porch." He swept a lock of hair out of his face and reconsidered. "Nah, just bury it.

Bury the whole damn thing."

"The bucket, too?"

"Jesus," he said. "Not the bucket. Leave the bucket in the barn."

He had driven off by the time I found the kittens under the bale; there were six, as white and lumpy as a box of ping-pong balls. Their bellies were round and distended by their mother's milk, no doubt, their eyes as red and swollen as mosquito bites on the shapeless knobs of their faces. Their ears were elaborately folded, like tiny pink origami. Some of them appeared to sleep; some squirmed blindly; a dozen red feet floated or squirmed in every direction.

I spread the pillowcase open on the bale and then, despite their muffled squealing, lifted each by its tail into the pillowcase, each seeming almost nothing and at the same time swollen, feeble, and weighted with life. As much as anything, I was thrilled and disturbed by the contact between my fingers and their hard, hairless tails as I lifted each of them from their reaching for the ground, four helpless feet spreading wide as each arched its neck, rising from the hole and attaching the exquisite, hideous splendor of their shape to an emotion held in check by me. I moved another and another and another.

I brought the pillowcase outside and looped it into a big knot. None of this was difficult, each gesture being simple in itself: drop them in the pillowcase; carry the pillowcase out and set it in the bucket; set the hose in the bucket; go to the spigot. My father's favorite hobbyhorse—*That's Just How It Goes*—was all the justification I wanted. The bucket was overfull by the time I got back from the spigot, the water running over. I pulled the hose and tossed it writhing onto the gravel.

I was unprepared though, for the yellowed pillowcase to have risen to the top and come half undone, sopping and bulged over the lip in a thick bubble, the fabric stained by a soapy scum, and for the miniscule chorus that rose up from inside as the mud around the bucket spread and darkened. I wondered what to do, where to stand, where to put my hands, until I remembered. I went back inside the barn, turned off the hose, came back and picked up the brick. I wasn't sure I heard them, their insect-like cries cruel to me in that moment. A milkweed spore floated past in never-ending slowness. What was grief, after all, but the cruelty released onto us by the sick and the dying?

I knelt and held the brick over the pillowcase, over the bucket, trying it out for size, a cuboid peg for a round hole brimming with icy water, conscious of the stupidity in my hands. Stupidity! Whatever I tried, however I turned it, I couldn't get the brick and the pillowcase to sink together. One end or another of the fabric rose up and I could hear their small dismay—I meant to drown them, not crush them. When I tossed the brick onto the grass, the full pillowcase surfaced. The water soaked my knees. At last, I poured out half the water and lifted the pillowcase by its neck and rewound it, releasing the bubble so that all it contained clotted together inside the fabric. I twisted the pillowcase more tightly and forced it under now and forced it down with both hands, the pail hard between my knees, and stayed leaning this way until the sleeves of my shirt and jacket were soaked to the elbows, until my wrists and my fingers ached from the too-cold water. I wished I'd understood before how cold it was, that water.

Sincerity is the Enemy of Love

Rosie buttoned her sweater while I went looking for her panties. The sky darkened a bit, the wind scattered a light rain. I zipped my jacket and sat next to her under a tree. She rubbed Mickey's ears and continued watching the meadow through the leaves. Mickey raised his head once and growled but remained, his forepaws crossed in front of him.

"What does he see?" she said. "Do you know?"

"No," I said, but he whimpered quietly and growled again.

"Is there someone there?" she said. "Someone who knows we're here?"

"A bear," I said. "Or maybe a mountain lion—a pack of wolves down from Ontario. Everyone here knows about us."

"Wolves?" she said.

"I don't know."

"Are you worried?"

"Sure. Could be your dad."

"Or someone who might rat on us?"

"Mr. Calvino and his entire sophomore biology class."

She smiled, taking that into consideration. She stared again at the trees.

"Whoever it is," I said, "if they were close enough to see us, Mickey wouldn't be lying there. Look, he's not even growling anymore. Whoever it is, is gone."

Mickey put his face down on his paws. Rosie put her hand on mine and leaned against me. I wanted to tell her again and again that I loved her, how much I loved her, that it had never been so clear to me that I loved someone—anyone—but I knew better. The woods were almost dark, almost cold by then, and for the moment we were almost perfect in our warmth together.

R

R crossed Guatemala and Mexico on foot and arrived in Revere, Massachusetts, when he was fourteen, having left his mother and younger siblings in the village of Mondoñedo where he was born. Sara, his mother, had a dozen children, mostly boys, all with a man who was married to a neighbor. Most of R's brothers had already made it to Revere and all of them, once settled, sent money to support her and her three remaining daughters. When he told me all this, he was seated in my office, eyeing me, holding a Red Sox hat in his hands, his work boots crossed at the ankles. That he loved his mother desperately was inarguable, though it had been twenty years since he'd seen her. She was too old and weak to travel and thanks to green-card regulations, none of them could go to her without risking their status. They hoped and prayed, mother and sons, being devoutly Catholic, for the day they would all come together. She was the most literate woman in Mondoñedo and loved to receive letters, he said, but writing was difficult and embarrassing to R and his brothers. He spoke on the phone with her every day, and refused to give up hope, even after receiving the news that she was sick.

According to the local doctor, who lived twenty miles away in San Andrés, she had stomach cancer. Modern treatments were not available, even in the capital. The doctor said he might help her using traditional methods, but it would cost three thousand dollars for certain expensive herbs. This was difficult for R and his brothers, all of whom worked as laborers and janitors, but they quickly wired the money. They kept in touch; they prayed with her over the phone, they visited their parish priests in Somerville and Revere, all of whom encouraged them to continue praying.

After six weeks Sara's condition improved, according to the doctor; it was a medical miracle! God loved Sara very much, the doctor said, but there had been setbacks. They had to restart the treatment, which would cost another three thousand. Again, they wired the money. After another month, they made a third payment. Everyone in their extended family, all the brothers and their spouses, were working two or three jobs. When the doctor made his fifth demand for the money, they began to argue; one brother lost his temper and made accusations. The eldest stopped returning phone calls. R feared they could no longer make the payment.

This was when he came to visit me, during a lunch break. We talked about the weather, his new night job cleaning at BU, how he walked with a limp because, when he was nine, a cow lay down while he was milking her and broke his leg. He mentioned his mother, the village of Mondoñedo, her small gardens, the cornfields, her pigs, the man who fathered him and all his siblings, and everything else he could think of in that moment related to her. It was a miracle how she had recovered, he said, quoting the doctor. The doctor and one of R's brothers insisted they try one more time. I knew what was coming, and yet I was surprised, too, helpless when he asked for help. What should I have said? That the doctor was a liar and a thief? That they had wasted fifteen thousand dollars? I gave him all the excuses: I was strapped at the moment, I had a family to support, I was a *blanco*, sure, but wasn't rich. I wasn't financially up to it, I said. *I wasn't up to it.*

Sitting in the kitchen with my wife that evening, we concluded my refusal was all there was to do.

"Maybe we could give them five hundred?" she said.

"Why?" I said. "For what?"

Three weeks later R phoned me. Sara was gone. He had wept and wept and wept, he said. They all had. He was a boy the last time her saw her. And he thanked me. He thanked me for my friendship, my kindness, my prayers.

James Stotts

boats

i pull away
just far enough
you're neither
here nor there
cool mornings
are coming
to the country
day by day
ghosts gradually
growing back
their winter coats
the stairs headed
headfirst
my way
like windows
in the way
of birds
do we never assume
nor break in
newer
less bloodied bodies
selves

the writing desk
you gave me
somehow

makes my smokes
taste sweeter
and so
might have
maybe made
a difference
but no
no one
anywhere ever
got over
anything
me over her
or you
any of us

pouring rain
on i-93
bulwarkcataract
channeling the heavens
over state 38
the switchyards and sullivan station
iron waterfall
i shelter under with the birds
and buses
and smoke and wait for work
i let the body learn its lines again
standing still
in its stall

my dance everynight is
a vain countersurvey
the caesars
will always
eventually
find us out
for what we are
i am
baryshnikov behind the bar
doing albrecht
by the grave
for the eye

that never blinks
and looks unblinking back
and documents the days

can i do this
to myself to death
late after
i lock the doors
my last camel's last breath is
living out its afterlife
on my lips
the spoils of the storm say
there's an easier way
reach down
for the stars
dive

defeat

maria is my shield
telling my stories for me
i rest her on my back
to sleep
she's so sweet
and when she's gone
my defense
against predators
is to make my body
poisonous meat
i am
you are
the world is
too much
conjugably
withholding

trek
labor day, tennis' u.s. open, 2018

lucky star to mahayana temple
past the navy yard the city as school

q on canal to grand central's
seven to flushing pilgrimage

drenched to the bone raqueteers
were dropping like flies on the grandstand

ferrer to nadal
and nadal to del potro retired

just as she was about to get her legs
our millenarian was rattled by the oracle

all the above cut their all
hear their hammers sucking air

do nothing by halves
the umbrella city's a satchel a spec

order me a honey dew on the rocks
boo no straw

Susan Barba

Night Painting

The infernal flicker of this city
gaslights strolling visitors,

tricks the river into thinking
its black ribbon is gem-embedded,

pearl lights, pale yolks, spilling skyward,
zygotes shivering in the waters.

The studio confirms this double
vision, attar of turpentine,

litany of chemical color,
spectral sight, as after sun.

Museum lawn of dew and cadmium,
Night and Day, the babies' heads,

giant domed dreaming sentries,
close- and open-lidded, twinned.

Emerald arborways unravel
homeward, the brick city not seen,

only ornate cornices, white
in the headlights, taillights red.

Morning, a dark chapel, brims,
amplified by bird cry.

Faint residue of the real,
pale watercolor wash.

Summer Birth

I saw the end that night in late July,
out on the lawn, bearing the pulse of pain,
that pain no man will ever know, which rends
enclosure, and the light comes pouring through.
Such darkness it is women's charge to carry,
through winter nights and mornings dark as night,
a temporary dark so final-seeming,
it overwrites the memory of day.
How strange that life begins with this eclipse
of self, and sorrow of apartness. Animal—
I curled inside the winter-long and leaned
toward spring, till sun broke over Boston and
the fuse inched green through buds and leaves and
    bloomed.
So love will pick the petals and we let it.

Marathon

Only the moon over Soldier's Field Road sees us depart,
quiet until the sun apocalyptic above the hospital
jars us into words at river's bend, electric pink
feedback feathering the water, mercury rising.
Last time I saw the sunrise I gave birth. Only the fittest
they've said should run and you're among them. Human
technicolor snakes and schoolbuses perambulate
the park and idly limber in preparation to go west
while in the garden an old man bends his knees and
    pushes air
with just his hands, slow as spring. The swan boats
out of hibernation sway, chained to the dock,
and a gray-skirted sneakered lady speedwalks through it all.
One day I'll wake this early of my own accord
and imagine where I'll go and meet me there.

Dispersal

driving the thruway
back and forth
that time of year
when the twin samaras
spun and sun found
harbor in the leaves

she felt the light slip
the more she strove

o

days ricocheted
from loss to loss

she read
tidal stress : tremor :: swarm : quake

she read
Exxon Mobil plans to Triple Its Bet
on Hottest Shale Field in the U.S.

she drove and drove
she snapped at the small ones
in the back she bracketed
misgiving

she read
Strong Risk of Crisis as Early as 2040

she was not speaking
to her neighbors
who'd razed the forest
next door for sport

she'd hoped for

equanimity

---

time

but there was only heat

o

re. space she wanted
nothing more
than a margin
undisturbed

re. time she wanted
never to accept it—

the trees succumbing
to storms with proper names

the grass succumbing
to polypropylene

she planted protests
but they were numbered

and the mayhem
was innumerable

o

she and I and you
and they and he

seeds

seeking
more than a life
in the wind

George Kalogeris

THE FUNERAL ORATION, 431 B.C.

The wagons are loaded down with their draped caskets.
The widows are holding back their lamentations.
The horses' hooves are restless in their restraints.

By the Tomb of the Unknown Soldier, the speaker stands
On a raised platform. But it's thanks to Thucydides
His voice will carry down through the centuries.

The Peloponnesian War has just begun,
Yet Pericles in his speech has already proven
Demokratía immortal—at least in the future

Perfect of Attic Greek at its glorious height.
Imperial Pallas Athena, her helmet uplifted,
Listens intently. There's nothing under the sun

As new as the Parthenon in its virginal marble.
Banished now the blind bard from the Polis.
Aesthetic Athens replaces Tragic Troy.

The City of Logos, whose gates are always open
To foreigners, especially those with nothing
To declare but their undeniable genius,

Is also the City of Eros, whose citizen-body
Will fight for their belovéd like an *erástes*—

A fiercely devoted, aggressive lover. The Spartans,

Of course, are formidable opponents. Consider
Their iron discipline, the honor-bound
Advance of their phalanx. But tribal insulation,

Compounded by suspicion of open spaces
Designed for open debate—a sunlit agóra,
Or Boston Common—will doom their way of life.

And now the most resounding lines of all:
"What we have achieved, my dear Athenians,
Will be an education for the world."

(Aglitter with dew is the grass at Gettysburg.)
And then, at the turn of a page: incurable plague.
Affliction, whose powers of articulation

Not even Athens can fathom, yet symptom by symptom
The spasms recorded in dense, Hippocratic detail.
And then again in dense, photographic detail.

Lucid the shrouded lens of Matthew Brady.
Grainy the film that crops the sprawling fields.
Turn the page and it's Whitman dressing the wounds.

"Impromptu" the hospital-church. Unspeakable
The lack of anesthetic. Torch-lit the tender,

Surgical helplessness of lyric precision.

And time and again as the ancient entropic cycle
Devolves, turning the Demos to Demogorgon,
Those massacres at Melos and My Lai.

But first that section on Corcýra's altars,
Murderously stained with the filial blood
Of the murderous suppliants that clung to them.

That primal section like a vivisection
Of Propaganda spawning Fanaticism
And all that flows in its wake, as honest speech

And common decency dissolve—and all
So purely distilled by all those verses beginning
With "and" in Shakespeare's sonnet sixty-six:

> *And needy nothing trimm'd in jollity,*
> *And purest faith unhappily forsworn,*
> *And guilded honor shamefully misplaced,*
>
> *And maiden virtue rudely strumpeted,*
> *And right perfection wrongfully disgraced,*
> *And strength by limping sway disabléd,*
>
> *And folly (doctor-like) controlling skill,*
> *And simple truth miscall'd simplicity,*

And captive good attending captain ill,

But *art made tongue-tied by authority*?
Not when the audience clamors for Pasternak
To read "the sixty-six" in their native Russian.

But first it's turncoat Alcibiades
In Spartan tunic, shorn of his flowing, luxuriant
Hair but not of his charismatic genius.

Enter Syracuse. The fleet destroyed.
The marble quarries packed with Athenians—
As if the whole endeavor were one big theater

Of Dionysus. *Total Annihilation*
Thucydides called it, quoting Herodotus
Accounting for Persian losses at Salamis.

The term redundant. The irony consummate. "Perish,
Enlightened by the vollied glare" writes Melville,
As the march into Virginia ends in the First

Manassas. And then again in Thomas Hobbes,
Translating *The Peloponnesian War* as training
For *Leviathan*, the work he pledged

To the Commonweal, and to his dear companion,
Sidney Godolphin, that "most worthy brother…

Unfortunately slain…in the Publique quarrel,

By an undiscerned and an undiscerning hand."
And then by implacable *then—O Captain! My Captain!*—
Set down in the grave, unfinished, exacting prose

Of the exiled general, Thucydides,
Lamenting his dearly beloved Pericles—
Forever lost to the Plague. And lost to the Polis.

ARCHIPELAGOES

Rosy-fingered dawn was over St. Lucia.
Ómeros had almost finished his epic.
But here, in Boston, he sat on a swivel chair

That faced the window facing the frozen river.
The Charles River. But then it was Lethe. And now
It's my teacher's shade that spins around and glares:

"Jimmy's dead. Poor Jimmy Baldwin's dead."
What did I know—a student who entered his office
Without an appointment—what did I know about rivers

"Older than the flow of human blood
In human veins…Ancient dusky rivers"
Still flowing through the lines of Langston Hughes?

And what did I know about that "austere and lonely"
Office that Robert Hayden's father kept—
As the poet slept—on all those winter Sundays?

I knew that Ómeros was Homer's name,
And it was the same in Modern Greek. I knew
My immigrant father had fought in World War II.

He too rose early, even on winter Sundays.
Into a mist will go the belief in harbors

Of an entire race, the Griot recited

To Derek Walcott. Into the rotting hulls
Of steerage the castaways had scratched their tribal,
Anonymous names. And out of that came *Baldwin*.

And over St. Lucia: rosy-fingered dawn.

Tope Ogundare

white ocean

in this white ocean, i am a brown body
bobbing, black hair tangled in *koko* waves.
i go to the barber's shop twice a month, determined
to shave away my difference. the doctor can't give
me anything for the melanin on my skin.

this body is not always a curse.
sometimes sticking out gets a sore thumb attention
& relief – the kindness of strangers, like cold
compress to a throbbing ache. strangers are walls
& holograms & mazes

& i lose the way into myself trying to find an in,
in this new world of cold sun
& familiar yet strange language.
here, my colours lose their 'u'
& 'u' is not in my neighborhood anymore.

time is on the wrong side too
in this often-tumultuous white ocean,
where i am a brown body fighting to stay afloat
buoyed by Twitter & Facebook & WhatsApp
looking into liquid crystal display for a lifeline

On Airports

airports are good for sightseeing
& storytelling.

a femme fatale sashays past,
dressed in black, down to her wedged heels,
sporting low cut hair dyed blonde.
an old man whistles
& winks at me.

a man sees his bride & turns red,
stops himself from running.
they lock lips eagerly beside me
& i turn red; such PDA is too heavy for me.
when love burns hot, it glowers & gleams.

a kid sidles up to her father
& he drags himself out from the world wide web
& beams a smile at her
sucking her into the whirlpool of love
in his brown eyes.

two men laugh loudly & hug,
slap each other's backs,
disentangle & walk in opposite directions.
a girl lingers in her mother's embrace
a second longer.

static from hidden speakers unfreezes the frame
& i feel like a voyeur caught in the act
& like my 6-year-old self, hand dripping stew
trying to explain the mystery of missing pieces of meat
from the cooking pot.

Autumn in Boston

Autumn in Boston
is a colorful painting on a grey canvas,
red & yellow & orange
are the colors of death.
the leaves thin out, fall to the ground,
like hairs from side effects of chemotherapy.
trees become skeletons with spindly arms
& take eerie forms under the street lights at night.

an ageing year bends under the weight
of passing time, leaves lose their luster of youth
& take on the color of aging
like silver strands that replace
blond & auburn hairs
telling tales of pastimes.

a deceitful lover, beguiling with bold,
bright, breathtaking beauty, superficial
charms & capricious weather.
an abusive spouse, wooing with flowers
& candies & sinister smiles
& winter's breath.

Autumn in Boston does not reveal
the brutality of the coming winter
but drops hints for the discerning.

i am too carried away with its beauty
to notice its fading sun, harsh winds
& cold hands.

Fred Marchant

A Bat in Mérida

Mid-summer and at night,
    I am floating on my back,

the pool in the courtyard,
    a sweet jungle scent in the air

when the bat angles in for a sip.
    The night is there to hide it,

to help it time and again skim
    the surface near my shoulder.

I take it as a sign of how
    the end of a life should be:

its swift arrival, with reason, need,
    and the softest graze,

a loving, almost comforting
    touch from another world

within the world we live in,
    a wing that feels like nothing else.

Jennifer Barber

Overdose

The light rain falling on the lake
wavers, more light than rain.

Three mallards slide into the shadows.

Two small boys wading with a net
shout to their mother,

There's a hole! The fish got away!

Blue spruce, blue dragonfly, the trick
of pretending not to know

what happened to Jake, my student.

The sun gets past a cloud.
The waves keep lapping at the dock.

The mother tells her boys to come on out.

No, we can't come out, not yet!

Postwar

The doctor who lived a block away
turned his basement into a bomb shelter.

I practiced my obstacle course:
climb the swing set, run down the slide.

My parents, like orphans, wouldn't say
what their childhoods had done.

I gave myself names I kept to myself.
I tested the trap door in the cellar floor.

My mother washed and folded our clothes.
My father couldn't catch her eye.

The storm lamp stood on the mantel,
joy and fear in its flame—

it guarded us against hurricanes.
Maybe if I squint, the flame's still there,

worlds ending, worlds being born.
The glass around the candle is my face.

Hermitess

I've grown old in this house
two miles from town.

At night the mice
run through the walls.

Their cries don't trouble me
but when a tree lets go

far in the night,
I think of my giant hemlocks

struck by the same idea,
shattering the roof,

barring the door and path.
Come morning, they're back

where they always were.
I am still myself.

Here, my anemones;
here, my patch of marigolds.

Elegy

The air around you, a silky skein
of blue and yellow thread.

Things giving way to other things,
the passing cars, the trees,

the skin of their leaves as thin
as eyelids letting sunlight through.

You walk into the heat of afternoon.
The houses watch you go.

You *are* the afternoon,
nowhere and everywhere.

Nobody hears you when you say,
Everyone was once someone's child.

George Saitoh

Six Portraits

1. Jerzy the Composer

He even commands his shoes, thought Jerzy, looking out through the centuries-old oozing panes at the twisted and curled up footwear of the hooded man in the parking lot taping the shattered windscreen.

Besides that new idea three earlier ideas were circling in Jerzy's mind: the unusual wall upholstery that was skins of red Anjou pear, avocado, and pomegranate; the notion that his mother's schizophrenia might have become resolved – both characters finally separated – in her two offspring which would explain, simply, why they could never get along; and that Jerzy had reprised his own body and its capacity for living at a time when most would consider it already well in decline, too late.

The last, of course, was the most fallible of ideas since its ultimate veracity resided wholly within one person: Jerzy, and, even more delimiting, within the short part of his life from when he had begun to compose. For who could say when his peak *would* have been, or when the upward or downward points of inflexion *would* have occurred had he begun composing earlier? (To do so would require roaming outside of Jerzy's and among the lives of others, including other composers, quite different from Jerzy who was unique). The fact was that Jerzy finally acknowledged his own talent – the disease the talentless are envious of, this umbilical cord that reconnected him to the world, (though there was really no 're' about it, it was the first time) – at 45, an age when regrets are more life-sustaining than conquests because they fuel what few may still lie up ahead.

But regret was not in Jerzy's repertoire, or anything so self-assured. In its place was wonder. And when he saw the figure outside in the sleet, stocky and despotically deft in the economy and rapidity of his movements about the car, Jerzy desperately wanted to allow him some talent too. A talent for fixing windscreens even, a talent for ignoring the cold, for repetition. Anything that he, Jerzy, felt incapable of at that very moment. Jerzy wanted to because the figure presumed it at all times, even now, in the present circumstances. It was simply a question of Jerzy guessing what that talent might be for that the man in the parking lot assumed was obvious, and then granting the recognition that was due.

The apparent divergence could be nonsense, Jerzy thought, as a heavy-set and bearded Jew plodded past in huge cushioned shoes, interceding between Jerzy and the man in the parking lot, breaking up his former idea. His trousers were rolled up to reveal short thick rabbi's shins. It was one of those ideas that could be supported or crushed in accordance with one's present outlook. Hadn't Vera's mother, Jerzy's grandmother, been a bimetal strip? And hadn't her nature appeared to resolve into the characters of Vera and her steel-hard brother, Jerzy's uncle

Robart, who told Jerzy one day that he would kill him if he heard him mention Vera's name again? Then what had happened? What was still happening? Was it a never-ending anastomosis from generation to generation that looked resolved, and neat, up to a certain point when the forking started anew?

For years now, since before he had begun to compose, Jerzy had been going the other way, as he called it; and now, seeing the segmental, choppy movements of the man outside he was somehow reminded of that fact so strongly that he weakened, physically, at the notion of trying to turn even a fraction toward the old way ever again, as he had had to do during the brief visit. The old way was the denial of his imagination. It involved a systematic, minute-by-minute purging so that he might better soothe his mother's sensitivity, a sensitivity now transformed into the incongruous fragility (that only Jerzy understood) of the man in the parking lot.

Tamp, tamp, tamp, tamp went the heel of the car-mender's hand in a dull staccato. Although the sound barely reached Jerzy's ears, it was amplified in his brain by his eyes and his helplessly vengeful imagination. The compression of time that brought the constraining past, and the deadening suffocation along with it, right up to the brink of the present, was incomprehensible. For Jerzy it was the greatest of all mysteries about this life even with his new perspective. Yet this perspective, from inside the psychiatric ward, was the one thing that he, Jerzy, and only he, seemed to command. And only because he had dared to seek it.

Outside, after he had finished taping up the shattered windscreen of the car, Jerzy's brother lit a cigarette and drove off. The loud rattle echoed off the surface of the windowpanes. It merged with the rattle of the serving trolley coming down the corridor that told Jerzy it was time for the main meal of the day. END.

2. The Bark Stripper

Even sober the dirt-bedded skin lifted for him from its smooth inner secret in a gush of granted pleasure. As long as the rot had already begun. And all the better if the seeped-through wetness was slime – not much, just a film was enough, but slime nonetheless – that put a sheen on the newly exposed alabaster limb, as if the wood itself were some giant pupa, variegated with alternating branch-butts and chocolatey arabesques whose crazy canals had been gouged by minute cannibalistic cousins that writhed in the daylight before his eyes like spastics.

The merchandise was ivory to Ivor. "Thunk!" went the latest tusk against the massing pile whose ends kicked up submissively, however plaintively, at the overcrowding that stole more of their already maimed dignity, not to mention majesty. (Nearby elephantine trees that were not taken entirely for ivory and cut up, stripped, and stacked *in toto,* stood stoic and amputated).

Wherever he sat the smoke choked him. The damp egg-infested bark smoldered with a chlorine-colored fume that swung and swirled until the whole pocket of the yard was a yellow haze of Autumn-scented mushrooms that, drunk, drunker, might have been pleasant, pleasanter.

The toes Ivor kicked with were swollen but not always painful, and the split down the center of his right thumbnail had dried up for good, it seemed, this time.

Only his left eye hurt, or bothered him (it didn't hurt as much as itch and irritate) though it was mostly his fear of blindness, already showing signs of descending, that worried him. There we have the role of smoke in all of this.

"Don't play with your food!" Ivor's mother used to whine. He was driven to thoughts of murder and even masturbation by her nagging. One time, when she began vacuuming after a biting put-down he went into the toilet she had just finished and released his angry penis, brazenly rolling the skin to and fro; the sickening sensation rose against the vacuum's soundtrack. But he had stopped in time, just before the moment when he felt certain he would have been swept down the toilet drain, all but his solid male item (even the clutching hand) in a mush of human disintegration.

He used to have crisps for lunch, with beer and bread, and look at his face in the mirror fragment for smoke stains, and examine his hands after washing them, when they stung, for sepsis. He would roll the eye-cack between both layers of lashes and throw water from the silver tap into his eyes to cool the balls down. And he would count things, his lucky stars sometimes if he were sober enough and in that frame of mind.

They sacked Ivor from his last job at the restaurant but he was never caught for burning it to the ground. And when, sometimes, he heard a creaking board that seemed to be overhead while he sat alone in his corner at night, he would wonder why. Had they been so stupid or had he been so clever? Or was it a matter of luck? Good or bad he daren't trifle mentally with. Who could say what a bark stripper was, whether one to envy or one to pity? Who could say? Who would be bothered to say? Who, if any, were the other bark strippers? Bark stripping was just the next thing to happen, like a redheaded baby.

"Heat it up you cunting bastard!" would sometimes stab his thoughts, all of a sudden, and make him feel naked, though he wasn't, holding his pretty little penis as it pumped up and up into a puce tip of shiny asparagus, though it wasn't. "Heat what up?" would flash in his mind in automatic response and he would peer over his shoulder though he hadn't at the original time. Then a stalemate. A detente sometimes, but never a rapprochement let alone a reconciliation. A stunning nothing in other words.

Ivor's hands would hold a million tiny needles when he squeezed them into fists, and then regretted the wasted energy he needed to save up, for he was chronically deficient, and had to be careful. It was the same for money. But now his money was all gone and Ivor was down to imagining the bark fibers were a reindeer jerky and the slime a bitter-wild seasoning that would sweeten in his mouth a second or two after swallowing, though it never did.

That ivory that Ivor gathered in sufficiently obedient piles was real ivory; and though his real name was not

Ivor, it should have been, even might have been, for all the contradictions and lapses his mother had been prone to. Snap, crackle, and pop saved his life as long as there had been a Rice Krispies box in the kitchen for him to look at. He never completely finished a box until there was a new one. Snap, crackle, and pop were made-up names, but they might have been the real names of the cheerful elves leaping out to greet Ivor with their tall Looney-Tunes eyes and thick quiffs. The bark strips went snap, crackle, and pop anywhere dry.

Ivor's naked body, when it was found, contained masticated wood fibers. But more remarkable, the newspaper article went, was that the penis was tied by a filament of unraveled rope to a bark-stripped tree-limb. That branch was buried amongst a pile upon which Ivor's body lay face down, embracing, in *rigor mortis*. END.

3. The Boxer on the Bus

"My enemies to the grave," he would remind himself stepping into the ring, and well before that, when training was first crystallizing into the hardness of routine. It was a cheap credo that he felt took away from him, from his character, somehow. But it was so effective just the same. "Their saber will always rattle for me, no matter what," he found himself capable of taking as fact, "so long as I am trying my best."

How easy it was for him to think while he was training. How *simple*. It reminded him of the bare trees in December, nude and pelted by wetness, at the very edge of worthless being, and enduring it until spring. December always came smack in the middle of two lovely Junes, not vice-versa, not for him, never during training. If December hadn't arrived during training, then it was approaching.

When it was over, and he had won, a woman would come near and set about touching him unpredictably and unexpectedly with her hands. It could last for weeks, but it was usually days before, constipated and unable to go back to sleep after waking around two in the morning, he would part from her. Once, it had lasted nearly half a year. The nearness was peculiarly unsettling, and though not purely unpleasant, its effect, or its potential (it seemed to manifest a potential), was impossible for him to fathom, though he never relented for a moment in trying. The touches in themselves were catastrophic, yet sometimes they were catastrophically pleasant. Like heroin, the touches carried a mysterious, if lighter, load of potential that couldn't be conquered through the medium of his own being. Through it all there would be the spurious mention of love.

The highlight of the day is often unpredicted and unexpected, and it could seem insignificant at the time and, without the proper degree of awareness, in retrospect as well. At least that is something he found he believed. Whatever form it took, it represented a moment when he both knew and felt known coincidentally; and it just came and went quietly, forgotten or else forever after remembered as capital to fend off impoverishment of the spirit. A special moment could alter one's life.

And so it had happened that day, the lazy December sun dragging itself skyward behind a barricade of rainclouds as he came out of the park near Reading Depot to take the bus. It was only to be warm: he had nothing in common with the other passengers, destination-wise. And yet his prejudices were to be curtailed. It had been cold overnight and his large hands, big as shovels, were still freezing compared with the warm felt of the seat he spread them upon, for all to see. There was no question he was getting older. His feet too were huge, like canal barges. And he was as tall as an adult. Only his muscles lagged behind, were out of step, the cause of his habitual self and public ridicule. It was ridicule he breathed as freely as air, and fully expected to find in the warm bus that December day, and didn't.

They were looking at his hands, of course, as they always did, but not with their usual faces. Indeed, they were interested, but they were not knowing, and they were not banded as one audience but were scattered, weak individuals. Looking at his hands each was troubled by a private mystery that, solved, could turn out equally to honor or malign them. Swelling red in the warmth, the grazed knuckles were raw from the thorns that, during the fitful sleep, he had flung them against the previous night. As he rubbed the knuckles of one hand with the fingers of the other and recorded every detail of the glances it drew, he somehow knew he should never forget them. END.

4. The Best (The Monomaniac)

It fell on a Tuesday this time, the powerful urge to achieve. After ten years in America he was used to it. As usual, he was prepared though not unsurprised. Being surprised felt like the most basic of human entitlements. The last one should give up. Surprises took him back to the defecations of a Peruvian childhood, the earliest in his memory, making him in an instant aware of the shortness of time, the span he had already lived through, and how young he still felt withal; that he had better hurry if he wanted to get something significant done while there was still enough time left. He tried to calculate how much time was left, then subtracted a fraction from the end to get the useful amount. There should be enough, he thought, if all goes well, if I hurry to make sure.

He released his wife last. She slipped off the primed surface of his brain like his friends a short time earlier, and like every other person on the planet he had ever had any relations with. But they would be re-instated later. It would be better if they knew that in advance but there was no time to waste on explaining. There was no explanation to offer in any case, and they would not want to hear it even if there was. They were not like him; he was certainly not like them. This is when it showed. He had grown tired of formulating apologies: apologies made no difference: he no longer bothered with them. Incompatibility was as much their fault as it was his, even if they were many and he was but one.

He remembered back to when they would devour his guilt, taking it for granted when it was offered up to them. It had been gorgeously insufficient for their appetites. It was different now, though. Still, he found himself wavering between fury and pity, towards them and also towards himself. It buoyed him like a cushion of flammable vapor, loosening him from what seemed to be moorings in preparation for take-off.

Alone and unfettered, his brain flowered possible approaches in unreadable abundance; a series of glimpses at what he might be about to do that he would never quite see again in the future, in the same light, whatever he did, however he ended up doing it. Like the people he knew, galloping time was beyond simple contempt for him now: it harbored the cold compounded resentment of a parent for a child they had not the courage to abandon, might eventually find a use for.

At the height of his exertion a warm moist wind, blowing for days from the Caribbean, had not yet broken apart the clouds in the thunderstorm it promised. The people sweltered in discomfort. The world's work seemed to pile up, waiting to be done, so much the uglier hidden from the sun's rays, like muck. It was work that was too much for the others to bear. He couldn't help himself laughing as he molded the clay from a blueprint in his mind that flowed like a stream.

Afterwards, he knew, he would rest and dream and

remember what he had done and what those he would by then have reinstated a certain regard for would think of it. He would share in their mystery, like a spectator on the fringe, but one who cares less than anybody about what has occurred, interested only in the crowd itself. It would bring some reward. It would lift him a fraction – nowhere near commensurately, but a little nonetheless; a little more than he had relied on when he was alone, doing his best. END.

5. Ich War

What had seemed during his first week away a cozy nest he was certain to return to was, by the second, already fading to a silhouetted memory. Yet the place he was currently staying still seemed foreign for all the work he did there, for all the accumulated time he was spending in it, for all the familiarity he ought to have been earning from his experiences. But while his efforts appeared to others as an unbroken stream, inside him its origins were continuously shifting.

During the first week he had been something of a professional, with a professional's detachment and small-set orderliness. The whims he had been known for appeared to him, if they really appeared at all, as inspirations. In any case his hands, sensitive and thin, felt a great deal and fed it all to his prepared brain without dispute. From his work there was ample cause for congratulations: he found he was humble enough to enjoy even the smallest.

Inside his mind two reels spooled parallel versions of the same images, just like a professional. During that first, sure, week he carried and projected both without fatigue, and with no conscious sense of duty, and together they minced the time of day into fine, harmless, and invisible dust. At night he had found himself smiling easily and open to any kind of slop, any sort of company, and he could absorb large amounts of strong spirits without ill-effect.

The doves and sparrows had been coming and going trailing nest materials in their beaks and, much more than at other times, seemed to be cocking their heads indecisively at certain moments as if to better follow the airborne instructions from Nature. It seemed to be the one time of year when their actions had to follow a precise format, within a narrow span of time, and their tension was of great amusement to him. Whenever they caught his eye he would condescend to them a few moments of attention, after which he would feel that blessed sensation of ampleness when one is at ease with two entirely separate worlds at once; worlds that are personally unharmful, neither having an exclusive claim of ownership. Unharmful because one is not a part of them.

Then the weather took a turn for the worse. They said that in 1945 it had rained for 23 days in a row. Could it happen again? The fog blotted out the opposite bank of the Charles River and, with the bridge-lights out, the prospect was reduced to the streaming slick of slow-moving water. Vehicle headlamps filled the air with grains of cold sand. The wool of garments furred and aged like the expressions on the faces he had known less than a month, and made him wonder at times if he were not in a place where time passed at a different rate.

On the fifth day of the drear, on his evening walk through Back Bay, slow diners observing him through the clean glass of expensive hotels, he passed a cake shop. When he stopped the large redbrick houses around him seemed to wheeze in their old age but remained perfectly straight and still. The shop was a half-story higher than the partially subterranean drinking parlors he now shunned. Through the glass the creamy-white interior resembled the surface of a cake itself, and the glass-hooded counter's contents, studded with deep-red berries, were few: it was a successful cake shop. The last pair of clients was stooped over, in no rush to return outside. The girl waited with a tiny sway and arms folded in a soft clutch under her large natural breasts. Her t-shirt carried the name of the shop: Sweet.

She saw him and smiled and her hair, tied loosely over one shoulder, coiled around her craning neck. Inside must have been well heated, the cake display case cooled artificially. She blinked slowly and held, he thought, her smile while turning back to the ignorant pair. He grew warm in the face and touched his own smile, the first in almost a month, and the shape was like a small boat. It reminded him of the boat he had made from scrap material taken from the dump when he was seven.

The silver coating coalesced into invisible water when he put his hand on his chest. 'Cupcakes' was all that he could make out on the menu hoarding over her fine big head, from so far away. END.

6. The Snowdonia Philharmonic Orchestra

He had always felt more European than American, wondered what it would have been like if his parents had stayed in the place where they were born, wherever that had been exactly, or gone to New Zealand first instead, where they might have found it more suited to their original character. It wasn't a small world after all, he had discovered. Rather, it was much too big.

Baile Atha Cliath was forged into the iron gates of the bubblegum-pink house he was guided to that blowy, warm, and showery dusk. It was late spring and the house was round as a button, its windows trimmed and glazed with a precision that was remarkable, even without the astonishing curvature.

'Pristine' was the word written in his head as he self-consciously, stupidly, entered, and used the wall to guide him, keeping it constantly in reach, thus approaching his hostess in an arc of ignorance befitting her smile. On the way, among other sights, he saw the blown-up framed photo of a white peak with grey and blue striations, curved halfway down perpendicularly to the horizontally curving wall that now made him shift from thinking of crannogs – round ancient Celtic lake-dwellings – to igloos.

"You've come," she confirmed. The low music seemed about to erupt in crescendo at any moment. They embraced and pressed hard, sopping tongues together almost destructively, using muscles at the base – deep inside the mouth – that satisfied a hunger when they ached with tiredness. Her breasts were squashed away, for her breastbone jarred upon his. Swords.

She tasted of warm meltwater. Somehow they both continued to breathe, using some other, minor muscles, somewhere around the ribs. It seemed to last 15 minutes but couldn't have. When they broke off it must had been his doing because her arms remained outstretched as he turned to regard the man he had arrived with: her husband.

On that same day, at the very same time, a wintry dawnlight covered the Shetland Isles, Western Ireland and the cap of Mount Snowdon, Wales, in a trigonometric fantasy. It was the perfect setting for the one act of his ordinary, though exceptional if you wished to think so, life that he would have no opportunity to reflect on afterwards; at least not in the only familiar, earthly, sense.

"It was dumb of me," one would surely confess then, setting a marker, when the news had begun to spread, bringing old friends back together again, apropos of allowing contact to lapse.

"It probably wouldn't have made any difference, but..." from another one, assuming a disproportionate amount of guilt in an effort to cast uncertainty on the sliver that was probably merited, merited perhaps to all who had been once close to him, and thus an ingredient in the net dissatisfaction of his experience.

"What banner did he fly under?" Who would ask that of him, now that the full clarity of the misapprehension of his character had manifested beyond question? Perhaps, in private, one or two. The ones he had held out most hope for a connection with until the very end; a hope he finally projected posthumously, using his imagination's last drops (it had worked up to the end). One...two... three. Yes, three at least would be saved by this. He would be saving them by granting them the event to experience up close, vicariously, on both sides of the great divide. It was something, among other things, that he was never granted and now never could be. Two of them probably – not three. One if he thought hard enough about it. But none if he thought too hard.

"It's the only game in town, kiddo," she quipped as they broke tongues again and he now pictured her New Zealand home as a soft-furnished lighthouse. The flames flying out from the thick log in the center seemed to rotate in a single direction. He was onto the word 'beacon' when she interrupted his thoughts with her... END.

Meia Geddes

An Investigation of Emerging Language

The history of the English language may be delineated into three periods: The Old English period, from the occupation of Great Britain in 449 to the Battle of Hastings in 1066, The Middle English period up until 1485 with the death of Richard III, and The Modern English period, up to the present day. As any scholar would point out, these dates reflect occurrences of a political nature and should be considered liberally. In attributing precise years to these shifting periods, one must observe that each melded into another, as prose might meld into poetry, and that the numbers simply cannot account for the countless, individual, overlapping instances of change, both grammatical and in regards to pronunciation.

Many figures in the history of English are renowned for their effect on its development. Alfred the Great indisputably altered Old English by standardizing the language into his West Saxon dialect. Bede the Venerable's *Ecclesiastical History of the English People* established a much-needed memory for the English-speaking peoples of Great Britain. Wycliffe's Bible of translated scripture infiltrated every home's bedside table. Caxton's printers imprinted every desktop. Dictionaries and paper proliferated, and people soon found themselves immersed in words. Saussure fathered structural linguistics, illuminated the arbitrary nature of language, and thus, of the world—in fact, one began to wonder if things other than language—that is to say, everything—might be suffused with the unreal.

Scholar James Robert Junior specialized in the aforementioned moments of arbitrary transition, from Old English to Middle English, Middle English to Modern English, and everything in between—Early Modern English, Late Middle English, and so forth. He had particularly distinguished himself in his studies of the relationship between nominative-accusative plural and genitive plural noun cases and their transition from Old English to Middle English. He had also received substantial critical acclaim for his contributions to the study of The Great Vowel Shift.

As Professor Emeritus of Linguistics and English Literature, JRJ found himself just where he wanted to be: immersed in declensions, surrounded by peers who knew that the acronym "IPA" stood for International Phonetic Alphabet, and speaking Old English to himself in the quiet of his small, papered office. JRJ spent hours in his office, often staring at his curtains enraptured. JRJ's curtains were made of a heavy velvet fabric, dark blue so that the light from the windows could not seep through. This relationship with his curtains may most accurately be characterized as one of symbiosis—just as a group of consonants and vowels will inevitably merge together to slip into the being of a word, so too did JRJ slip into the velvety folds of his office curtains. When JRJ was not carrying on with his curtains, he was receiving students during his office hours with great delight. However, he never quite seemed to realize that they could barely see him. Both professor and visitor sat in the darkness of lampless times.

JRJ had traveled to many places in his life and loved to discuss the various dialects and linguistic quirks of those he had encountered. He could name the dozen ways an "r" might present itself, saying with great empathy, "An incredibly difficult thing, the "r"—real slippery, a very slippery being." For JRJ, letters were very much alive; one simply went about birthing them in various ways from the mouth. So, JRJ would like to say that he was constantly giving birth, each and every day, and that he simply could not help himself, nor did he want to.

JRJ aimed to be an amiable man. He unhinged himself in order to open doors for others. He suppressed his trumpeting nostrils employing his monogrammed handkerchief. He always washed his hands and laughed at the right times. He cleaned the dirty undersides of stacked dishes. In all eyes, JRJ was an accomplished success of a man. If there was one dilemma he faced in life, it had to do with his wife. To be fair, this was a dilemma that JRJ and his wife shared after thirty-eight years of marriage.

The history of JRJ and his wife may be delineated into several time periods: The Romance Period, from May flowers to December deflowering, The Engagement period, from a ring in November to another in April, and The Marriage period, from 1976 up to the present day. In retrospect, these periods did not precisely adhere to actual events—the one-day Break, for instance—but for the sake of simplicity and ease of telling, this translation of time allows one to move forward.

JRJ took great interest in the transitionary details of his relationship with his wife: their first kiss, their first date, their first time in bed, and so forth. As one may differentiate indicative, subjunctive, imperative, and participle verb forms in the present and preterit tenses, so too was JRJ's marriage demarcated. Of course, all of these seemingly different forms indicate precisely the same thing—a verb, a love—but still, JRJ took note of this information in a large ledger with a precision that would astound even the lady herself.

The ledger was quite complex—a veritable beast, in fact, to the outside observer. JRJ felt that the ledger erected a temporal history for himself and his wife, a history approaching that of Bede the Venerable's *Ecclesiastical History of the English People* in dignity, solemnity, and grandeur. It granted form and gravity to a relationship of unknown magnitude. The first, left-most column noted the month, date, and year of the relationship development in question. The second column represented the duration of this development, a rough estimate in seconds. The next column featured a mere phrase, a description, the development itself, to be expanded upon in the fourth column dedicated to detailing that occasion as precisely and literally as possible.

Now it must be noted that not everything could be deemed a development. For example, JRJ had to decide whether kissing for the tenth time constituted a development worthy of recordation. Such decisions distinguished the great histories from those that became history. JRJ decided that in this case, as with reconstructed Indo-European words, it was best to hazard an attempt at documentation than have none at all. The tenth kiss found its way into the ledger.

A spacious fifth column allowed space for JRJ to examine the subjective feelings and thoughts that accompanied the documented facts of his experience with his girlfriend-turned fiancée-turned-wife, or more precisely, the immediate feelings and thoughts of the moment, nothing more and nothing less. The sixth column aspired to a more diachronic approach to the experience, examining JRJ's feelings and thoughts in the larger context of the couple's long-term relationship. Of course, JRJ felt a great desire to explore the possible feelings and thoughts of his wife in a speculative seventh column, and so he did this briefly; however, he believed quite strongly that only his wife could know what she felt and thought, and that the seventh column was more of a personal game, almost a literary exercise, slipping into another's shoes for a time to gain perspective on himself more than anything else. Not that this slippage was an act of egotism; rather, it never hurt to have multiple vantage points to see oneself in. Just like one might examine the similarities and differences of hundreds of cognates, slowly discovering that each contributes to an overwhelming sense that there is greater overall similarity than contrast. Finally, in the eighth column of the ledger, JRJ explored his own potential feelings and thoughts in light of his wife's potential feelings and thoughts. He chuckled at this exercise in meta-analysis, finding no end to his delight.

Every week, and often almost every day, JRJ would update his ledger, completely immersed, carefully reflecting on his relationship with his wife while she occupied herself with other matters. Indeed, as far as JRJ could see, his wife was unaware of the nature of his ledger. This was because JRJ's wife was blind. She also was deaf in the left ear. Sometimes, JRJ had to say things twice, even a third time, for her to hear. When this happened, JRJ would sometimes repeat himself and try again in Middle English or Old English and she would understand him more easily. As JRJ would be the first the point out, Modern English had evolved into an extraordinarily lazy language, letters sliced every which way in a desperate and degenerate movement for maximizing ease of articulation. JRJ's wife, on the other hand, could be deemed neither lazy nor inarticulate.

Among other rare qualities, JRJ's wife possessed both

extraordinary intelligence and extraordinary feeling. This was why he had fallen in love with her. The pair had met on a ship, and on the slippery, salty deck, the two promptly launched into a linguistic debate of such wind and fire—on the advantages and disadvantages of the diachronic and synchronic approaches to linguistics—that they knew and quite rapidly verbally agreed that they must one day marry. In a sense, then, JRJ and his wife made a marriage that day. JRJ pointed out that they were like two parts of a compound word—of course they could find other syllables, but the word that *they* formed was like no other. JRJ's new love thought this very silly and lovely, if not entirely accurate.

JRJ secretly thought it a definite merit that his wife could not see, for he was a rather unattractive man, on the border of ugly. Of this he was painfully aware, and he dutifully and honestly informed his wife of this fact quite soon after they met. In fact, he went into far greater detail as to his anatomical shortcomings than was necessary or probably appropriate, but she assured him that only his character and fidelity mattered. JRJ felt extraordinarily blessed to have found such a woman. Not only was she of good character and loyal herself, but she was also rather beautiful. Closed and often half-open eyes gave her a sleepy, though endearingly dreamy quality.

Their first night together was better by far than even The Great Vowel Shift. Things within JRJ's body shifted in such marvelous ways that he wondered why he had spent so many hours at a desk when he could have been lying in bed. Being blind, JRJ's wife—soon-to-be-wife at the time—had excellent possession of faculty in realms other than the eyes. In other words, she made use of her touch and voice with a greater-than-average lack of inhibition. JRJ was the beneficiary of this. He simply had to wrap his arms about her waist and she would heave a great sigh and sway with desire. Likewise, to JRJ, the touch of her hand was like a gently placed fricative, soft and soothing and hinting at something open, something unendingly splendid.

When they conversed, each covered such difficult and vast territory to the other, topics of such obscure nature, that it often seemed they spoke different dialects altogether. Yet somehow, they always met in the middle, found a language of metaphor and simile and anecdote that transcended mere syntax, semiotics, lexicon. They inhabited one another's conversation as if with their bodies. Neither quite understood how this miraculous connection worked; it simply was the kind of chemistry that cannot be affected. JRJ's wife often told him that she felt undone by the power of even a handful of his words.

This is why, when, on that fateful day when JRJ's wife told him that a man who was not her husband had made love to her by an accident of fate, JRJ promptly documented this fact in his ledger and then fainted. An hour later, he awoke to darkness and looked into his wife's ever-closed eyes. He asked if it truly had been an accident, for he would not ask again. JRJ's wife assured him that yes, it had been a mistake, the ending act of the caressing touch of a hand. JRJ nodded, updated the ledger, and went to bed beside his wife. They fell asleep in peace, and during the night her hand slowly drifted to rest upon his belly, a great big voiceless question mark, an unsure 's' drawn across his torso in a state of both declaration and withdrawal. The air weighed heavy with the unsaid.

JRJ lay thinking about King Alfred. Ah, what a man was he! "How was this man? Was he as good as me?" he mumbled to his wife. Had this stranger managed to bring JRJ's wife to realize the full range of high, middle, and low vowels, including but not limited to front, central, and back? JRJ told his wife he hoped this other man had not let her down, and that if so, and even if not, JRJ would rectify this. The hand of JRJ's wife stilled, like the tremor of a little 'y,' hesitating between consonant and vowel, movement and sleep—but she did not respond.

The following morning, JRJ moved his hand over hers and whispered "Gloria." She awoke, and something between the said and the unsaid spoke. JRJ found himself embracing his wife, felt an overwhelming sweetness, so sweet, oh yes, "O," he said, and he found himself uttering a mixture of Old English, Middle English, and Modern English. Gloria led him to his ledger to record this moment of birth, or maybe it was rebirth, and they went to bed again and again and again.

*Informed by lectures from English professor Lesley Jacobs and *The Origins and Development of the English Language, Seventh Edition*.

Liz Sux

Liz Sux 237

Pınar Yaşar

immigrant // refugee, childhood // fantasy

red-tipped linen worn summers in the kitchen
eating fruits, words that look like seeded disputes

between caution and melancholy,
pistachios in the yogurt, snow in the measuring spoons

for each feverish night, coffee in a shadow,
coffee in a pot blooming with delight

at the sugary sensation of recycling debts,
sweeter each generation the echo of regret

when they said,

// "just tell me where they are"
// "tell me who you are"
// "this is all you are"

swirl myself around, reuse words because
language is my only power (for) now.

conceptualineage

tragedy as beneficial
to fear, armchairs full of
religious zeal, disguised as people
disguised as planets
flattened to chaos, calling it
god's plan when it should be
called a fast food chant, easy
in the breeze of language
grazing the overgrowth in each
wide shot
of nature and metal at odds
(as though they are not the same),
cheap bullets and cheaper fame
in hundred dollar bills like kings
feasting on promises
to excuse the overdue tax payments,
give each family a single rice grain
in exchange for the heads
that populate
instagram feeds,
hometown buffet,
stacked conveyor names
plucked like cover ups
when the belt rolls
this way.

Elke Thoms

Poe's Commute

A still blur down Charles Street,
Poe flees the city that shamed him.
As he leaves, he can tell I am posting a picture
of the Garden
with a caption borrowing his words—
a tidy quote for this millisecond mood.
Last night I met a man,
and even though when I passed Poe yesterday,
I didn't know him,
I now would like him to feel I am well read,
even on a Friday afternoon commute.
The photo I take, it is shining, hopeful—
Poe must run.
Maybe he believes
I should flee too.

Cardboard Square

We didn't, but sometimes I would
imagine making love
in your Beacon Hill apartment.
A rundown shoebox that must've belonged to a wealthy
 family's
cook, butler, or maid
80 years before it belonged to a college student
and his first taste of freedom.

We spent the year of record snow
On the all-organic mattress your mom insisted upon,
it activated my asthma more than any IKEA bed.
We'd wrestle with our upbringings
and then switch on the thermostat,
which was just for show.

I'd wake and stare at the door—bolted—with the 4" by
 4" window
looking into your neighbor's room.
I would scrutinize the small piece of cardboard
framed in Scotch tape, hiding the view—
a little Band-Aid wedged
between us and the outside world,
like the clothes we chose to keep on.

Tenor of the Esplanade

The glint of the water
on the Charles River Esplanade
makes a sound like new nylon
as you sit, restringing the guitar
my first love gave me.

This evening, I am content.
Unlike the strings
you struggle with on my behalf,
these lines I play with
are writing themselves.

Stephen Sturgeon

C.O.P.S.

I

The next morning I went to get some clothes.
They arrested me. Pharaoh's transom shadows—
though you have appreciated a brain juggler—
old things about to get thrown away.
A lot of people want to know who you are,
if there are sun spots on m'lady's teeth
traveling to a friend's house, smiling like a dream.
Shall we tell them, you are one born under
synonymous signs, a replicable anomaly,
fissured garbage, cooked by your own goose?
Matricidal. OK. Cruciform blades
hovering, like a parallel zenith.
What. Kids falling out of automobiles,
no taste at all that way, they arrested me

II

Window management. Cloud management.
Speed of light management. The mudlifter.
I am sitting in a room. Millions of things
are happening, a newspaper falls down
the stairs, my son picks it up, and he reads,
It is worse to have marriage problem unmarried.

Tired with these, it's technics: nature's
catastrophe, weather on the moon,
he's funny to dress like a cavalier
and walk up to people with no clothes on.
Weekend cooking? After the cinema
it's an oft-looked-forward-to thing. Tell Ben
I say I'm sorry for everything when I'm gone.
I told him but tell him when I'm gone.

III

One cannot climb through such mountains of juice
without feeling exercised. I am not
the only one to see in surround-sound
crescent trees and gelded alligators
flicking into focus on extrasolar
planets. Masks can be someone's fabulous friends
forever speaking in repulsive accents.
Sentencing such a criminal, keep in mind
histories of the visi-goths, his glare
unrepentant and befitting the number
one killer of Seal Team Six heroes.
Among royalty everyone is family
until the Queen drinks her last glass of port…
leaves the door open a sliver… lamps switch off

Nate Klug

OURSELVES

Digging at Half-Moon Bay,
the dog dreams too hard--

a rattle of tags
near our legs in bed,

and sleep's last sneaker
wave breaks. All the way

until speaking, lying here,
you and I might

lay waste to or create anything,
little tyrants without names

passing pasts between each other.
But day's first words

arrive like nets, flung
from somewhere behind

our heads. We can hear the worn
rigging catch, involuntary

as animal muscle,
assuring us who we are--

rooted, fooled,
to this side of the shore.

BOSTON POST ROAD

I'm in her front seat heading home from school,
a stranger's car, a family friend's best friend,

it having been told to me in a hurry
early that morning that she'd know the way,

with something stumbling in their explaining
which told me too how, just like that, I could be lost,

so when we pass the familiar turn, the moment
doesn't even happen fast, and the longer now I wait to speak

the farther away we're getting, the farther back
both of us would have to go, and so I don't

because construction, or a detour, the driver
armed with reasons I would understand but can't,

or probably I never paid enough attention
to these dark town greens and peeling steeples in the past

and we're right on course, judging by her humming
and chat, home in time to sneak TV, or fumble through

a few drawers upstairs, before the others return
with their kind tired voices, their sounds for my name.

Stephanie Burt

AFTER CALLIMACHUS

One of the Muses took this singer,
in early childhood, onto her lap
and he never got up, or even stood up
after that. His failure
to cry or protest then
now seems, to us, a kind of harbinger.
Only in her arms, or on her semi-divine
ground, would he ever feel secure.

(fragment 471)

AFTER CALLIMACHUS

Ash from Marblehead, who made
his money in shipping, built
this temple to Demeter, with its food bank
and its shelter, seven beds;
but Timothy from Cambridge, out of guilt
or in order to thank
the goddess, or to placate
his socialist fiancée, since he won't quit
his job in finance, said he would commit
to keeping the temple solvent forever instead.

(Epigram 40)

Cassandra de Alba

on the back of an old disaster

silence so thick it's sexual

and a high whine of insect wings

in the fruit trees outside

I've lied already, they're city maples

but isn't it nice

to pretend at the pastoral,

isn't it nice to imagine

that the earth might nourish us

after all?

the water will rise over every street corner

I've ever kissed you on eventually

eventually there will be no one alive

who remembers my poems

but for now let me imagine

there are cows beyond the window,

lowing as they do into the spring night

let me imagine rows of sharp-leafed mint

and bright ofrenda marigolds

let me imagine a whole orchard

where we do not have to be afraid

Sarah O'Brien

Getting Carded

A hundred green lamps illuminate
uncomfortable chairs that creak
against wooden floors, spurring
stares from city dwellers.

Dark thighs on this fountain statue of a woman
fascinate tourists. They need every angle.
So this must be Boston, they nod.
Some more than others.

A pretty blonde reads an inscription
to get close to a boy wearing shades
on this definitely-cloudy day,
before wordlessly walking away.

I'm beyond the point, already
deceased from exhaustion.
Mourners gather at this library.
In lieu of flowers, *read books.*

When water ceases to spurt
most disperse. The boy's shades now sit
atop his head. The elephant in the poem
has left the room, taking my sanity with her.

It's nice to shiver in courtyards,

courting emotions best left
untouched while wondering how often
a bird cries.

Let music fill your ears—
we make it back in time
to joke about when I was carded,
fake ID confiscated.

You tease me for sending
that greeting card to your office,
a conquest after years of silence.
Each stamp is you drumming in my chest.

My Back to Boston

I am sleepy
after packing solo,
stuffing boxes
from the liquor store
into his silver Nissan
until visibility's laughable.
There is no feasible way
to hug the sunrise.

I almost die in Ohio;
raindrops assault the windshield.
We take the nearest exit, get high,
eat at a dead cow joint.
A man at this Missouri motel
gives us hard lemonade.
We do not have sex here.
We hear people moaning.

In another room, a baby sobs.
I miss a job I hate;
after work, Mike has food
waiting.
We fight or make love
or watch TV drama,
but it feels more real
than these country roads.

Patient Fingers

After Leonardo makes me pasta,
he scoots out the door to go clubbing
in the Southie side of Boston.

It's okay because I go to see you,
reclining on a terrorist watch list
just for your given middle name.

Fuck your perfect music taste.
I'll off-key this one later
as water warms my lonely.

My black thong brags sex.
You show me your sketches.
I show you my boobs.

I'm not embarrassed anymore;
not trying to be anyone's good girl.
I'm here for personal pleasure.

I show you how I roar,
how sweet
I shake.

Katia Kapovich

The Birch

The birch tree here has pierced her golden ears
and wears a kerchief
with stripes and dots in the exact same manner
as all white birches.

What foreign nation's northern wind has sent you
deep under cover,
distinguished lady, seeker of adventure,
mysterious lover?

When she, off the mid-fall flea market rack,
tries on some gold-cloth thing,
pulling closed the long zipper on her back,
it is life-changing.

Ryan Napier

"The Charles"

Last winter, I wrote a short story called "The Charles."

It was about a couple—a man and a woman. One summer day, the couple rent a kayak and paddle down the Charles. They enjoy themselves and decide to keep the kayak past the allotted time. They paddle and paddle, each spurring the other on, and as the afternoon passes, they come to feel that the world outside the kayak does not exist, that the universe contains only them and their happiness and the river. But when the sun goes down and a cold wind blows over the water, the man and the woman shiver and understand: they have to go back. They paddle silently through the darkness and return the kayak, and after paying for the extra rental time, they descend into the busy T station.

The story was fiction. I wasn't in a relationship. I had never even been in a kayak. "The Charles" was a meditation on the transitory nature of experience—or something like that. It wasn't my best story, but it had some good sentences.

I sent it to a bunch of literary journals, which rejected it. I tried other journals, and finally, in July, one of them said that it wanted to publish "The Charles" in its fall issue.

In the meantime, I had met E.

It happened at a party in Somerville—a couple dozen grad students and young professionals crowded into a small, weedy backyard. I knew most of the people there, but not the tall woman with short black hair. As a group of grad students complained about their advisors, I saw the tall woman roll her eyes, and when I was sure she was looking at me, I rolled mine too.

We ended up together in a corner of the yard overgrown with ferns and climbing vines. She explained that she had recently moved to the area for law school; I told her about my day job and my freelancing.

"Someone told me you write," she said.

"Barely."

She waited for me to say more. I didn't.

"Is it a secret?" she asked.

"It's not interesting enough to be a secret."

I texted her the next day, she texted back, and things progressed from there. She wanted to get to know the area, so as we walked around Cambridge and Somerville in the evenings, I pretended to be a tour guide, making up facts when I didn't know any real ones. She guessed which facts were real and which weren't, and she was usually right.

Her roommates hadn't moved in yet, so she had an entire apartment to herself. Soon, I was spending two or three nights a week there. It was August now, in the middle of one of those suffocating Somerville heat waves where the power goes out for hours and the sidewalks bake and crack. Her apartment didn't have air conditioning, and when it was too hot to sleep—which was often—we lay in her small bed, naked or nearly naked, drowsy and amiable, passing the time in various ways until sunrise.

The heat wave dragged on, but E. and I didn't mind.

One boiling afternoon, we went to Harvard Square for ice cream. All the seats in J.P. Lick's were taken (a Chinese tour group had come in before us), so we brought our cones down to the Charles, sat on the shore between the two bridges, and tried to eat the ice cream before it melted on our hands. It was cooler here than in the square, so after we finished our ice cream, we lay on the grass and looked at the river. Geese floated on the water, and the sunlight glimmered on the big sycamores and the orange tiles of the boathouse.

"This is a pretty spot," E. said.

"There's a Borges story set here," I said. "I think it's called 'The Other.' It's about Borges meeting his double. They sit on that bench over there and talk about other literary doppelgangers."

"No way. Fake."

"It's true. Truly. And that bridge to the right? That's where Quentin Compson kills himself in *The Sound and the Fury*."

"And here I was thinking it was pretty. I didn't know it was *literary*."

"Good thing you have an expert to show you around."

She rolled up her shirt to tan her stomach. A couple of yellow kayaks came around the bend.

"Looks fun," said E.

"You can rent them in Allston. I was supposed to go once, but it rained."

"We should do it sometime. Before my classes start."

I had no reason not to agree.

The next Saturday, we woke up early and took an Uber to Allston. We rented a double-kayak, put on the orange vests, and paddled east. E. was in the front seat, and as we worked up the river, I watched the churn of the muscles in her shoulders.

After a while, we passed under the BU Bridge and came into the wide part of the river. The sky was cloudless, but there was a steady wind, and for the first time in weeks, I felt cool. We decided to drift. E. took off her sandals and put her feet up on the hatch of the kayak. Some kids waved at us from the bridge, and we waved back. Ahead of us, Boston shimmered in the heat, and its reflection shone on the surface of the river.

One of the churches in Beacon Hill chimed—one o'clock. I said we should probably head back: our rental was due in an hour.

E. sighed. "I could stay out all day. Wouldn't it be nice to watch the sun set from the river?"

"We'd get tired though, paddling all day.

"We'd take turns. We'd go very slow."

I smiled. "You couldn't paddle us both."

"Of course I could." She flexed and made me feel her arm. "I was doing most of the work."

When we docked in Allston, our arms and shoulders ached, but the exhaustion was satisfying, almost pleasant. No bed was ever as soft as hers was that night. As we fell asleep, I could still feel the bobbing of the kayak.

A few weeks later, "The Charles" was published online. I debated whether to tell E.—but what would I tell her? The story wasn't about her, but if I told her that, it would look like I had something to hide. Besides, she probably wouldn't even read it. My stories never got more than a couple of likes.

That evening, I heard from E. She had seen "The Charles" on my Twitter. She sent me a long text.

I wrote back and explained the coincidence. The story didn't have anything to do with her or me. It was about the transitory nature of experience—or something like that. I asked if I could come to her apartment and talk about it in person. She said she needed some time.

We met a few days later at Bourbon Coffee. I bought us iced coffees and explained the whole thing again, taking out my phone to show her the date-stamps on my Submittable account and the acceptance email. I apologized for not warning her. We sat next to the window, and as we spoke, another version of us, mirrored in the glass, carried on the same conversation.

"You could have changed it," she said. "Or asked them not to publish it."

I hadn't thought of that. It was hard enough to get a story accepted once.

"Maybe I should have," I said. "I didn't handle it right. It was too weird for me to get my head around."

She sipped her coffee. "It *is* pretty weird."

I texted her that evening and again over the weekend, to no response. Several times, she started typing, but stopped. Finally, it came—another long text. She said that school was more work than she anticipated, and this wasn't the best time for her to be in a relationship, and she was sorry.

I couldn't help myself: I wrote back and asked if her decision had anything to do with "The Charles."

She replied quickly: "Yes."

She said she knew that I hadn't written it about her—but somehow, that made it worse.

I saw her point.

Porsha Olayiwola

Boston Ode

can you name a love without rigor? without sweet ache
and stretch and sunshine and sweat. Boston, parent of
our hallowed america, someone else's god before the

land was conquered. not the city we are born of, but it
is a charitable home. the same way the city upon a hill
gave birth to a country and we are all now inside a nation

and unbelonging at once. there is not a love i can fathom
with neither push nor pull. with neither grit nor sorrow
nor glory raining out the other end. what is a home, then,

if unhinged and locked. beloved city, gemmed with
bodegas on its corners, each studded with a cat guarding
the front stoop. gracious current, ringing the rush of the

river, the calm of the pond, and the guilt of the ocean
hushing secrets along dorchester's shores. beantown,
the best to keep the kept. slades on tremont and bintou's

in roslindale. home is the booth we plop into, the cafes
where the cashier craft meals that fill us. dear city,
southwest corridor thumming from the subway racing

against air. *patron saint of travelers*, plague of trolleys,
hold us still at lights, unlearn us bustle and hand us

patience. memorandum to slow. remind us who it is

we are and the blood love it took to raise us. city of
building blocks, *place of clear water*, of culture-
shaping, of planting and planning. *tri-hilled city*, tip

the cup of tea and bring on the massacre. city of
building up, up, up and people out, out, out. city of
ramming, city of running, of shifting, pacing, fast,

gone. champion of all. parade for everything.
celebrate the house, the keeper of our bones. nest
to our families. who will want if we won't and what

is a heart if it does not pulse? doesn't pull itself
toward itself and extract itself away again? what
is a heart if it doesn't pause then continue as to

remind the body it has chosen to keep going.
the gallant and the trodden, the gentrified and
the migrant. from roxbury to the seaport. harbor,

castle island, cobbled stoned tomb of chest, cobbled-
stoned town, always shouting our melancholy big
on your pavements, always chasing friends away

and further into your arms. sirened city, sunned
bathe, sillied picnic, public garden concerts. you

beautiful summer. you firework and worth it all.

you cold heat to my head, investor in wealth and health.
eldest master, first future of our states, teacher of love
long-standing, of might, fight and force. politics and wind

blow a barbed breeze, cutting kisses across the face. o'
city i love, o' city i know and walk the lawn of. city i
carry between my cheeks, around my neck. city i found

along my palms, under my nails. city of song blaring,
of loud leaping rhythm familiar and enescable, calling
out to each of us by heart, singing out to all of us by name.

Paul S. Rowe is an editor at *Queen Mob's Tea House,* Pen and Anvil Press, and Rhythm and Bones Press. His edited books include *The Taletellers* by Peter Caputo (Pen and Anvil Press 2020) and *Voices for the Cure: An Anthology By People Living with ALS and their Caregivers* (Rhythm and Bones Press 2020). His own writings on literature and music appear in *PopMatters, Literary Imagination, 3:AM Magazine, Empty Mirror,* and *Boston Hassle.* His poetry appears in *Moonchild Magazine, Salamander Magazine, and Hawk and Whippoorwill.* Paul lives in Byfield, Massachusetts with his wife Jessica and cat Clementine.

Ed Simon is an editor at *Berfrois* and a staff-writer for *The Millions*; his writing on literature, culture, and religion has been published in several different venues. His most recent book is *Furnace of this World; or, 36 Observations about Goodness*, available from Zero Books.

Peter Caputo (1950 – 2013) was Professor of English at Suffolk University in Boston for thirty-one years. His areas of expertise included 19th century English literature, history of the novel, classical mythology, and post-Jungian (archetypal) psychology. He is the author of the fiction collection *Saint Medusa* (Pen and Anvil Press) and was a finalist for the prestigious Peter Taylor Prize and semifinalist in the William Faulkner Competition for his forthcoming novel, also from Pen & Anvil Press, *The Taletellers* (Pen & Anvil Press). At the time of his passing he was at work on a second novel.

Susan Rich is the author of five books, most recently, *Cloud Pharmacy*, shortlisted for the Julie Suk prize, honoring poetry books from independent presses. She is the winner of the PEN USA Award for Poetry and the Times Literary Supplement Award, London. Her poems appear in places such as the Academy of American Poets *Poem-a-Day*, *Harvard Review*, *New England Review*, *Southern Review*, and *World Literature Today*. She is cofounder of Poets on the Coast, a yearly writing retreat located in La Conner, WA. She can be found on-line at thealchemistskitchen.blogspot.com. Her poem in this book "The Mapparium" was previously published in her book *The Cartographer's Tongue* (White Pine Press, 2000). Her forthcoming books include: *Gallery of Postcards and Maps: New and Selected* (Salmon Press) and *Blue Atlas* (Red Hen Press).

Ruth Lepson is poet-in-residence at the New England Conservatory of Music. Her books are *Dreaming in Color*, *Morphology*, *I Went Looking for You*, and *Ask Anyone*, and she edited *Poetry from Sojourner: A Feminist Anthology*. Her poems and prose have appeared in *Jacket 2*, *Ping Pong*, *Talisman*, *The Battersea Review*, *spoKe*, *Let the Bucket Down*, and many other publications.

Sassan Tabatabai is a Boston-based poet and translator. He is the author of *Uzunburun: Poems* (Pen and Anvil Press, 2011) and *Father of Persian Verse: Rudaki and his Poetry* (Leiden University Press, 2010).

Philip Nikolayev is a poet and literary scholar living in Boston. He is a polyglot and translates poetry from several languages. His poetic works are published in literary periodicals internationally, including *Poetry*, *The Paris Review*, and *Grand Street*. Nikolayev's collections include *Monkey Time* (Verse/Wave Books) and *Letters from Aldenderry* (Salt). He co-edits *Fulcrum*, a serial anthology of poetry and critical writing.

Raquel Balboni's first collection of poems is *XXX Poems* (Art & Letters, 2020). Her poems have appeared in *The Brooklyn Rail, SpoKe, Dig Boston, The Cafe Review, Art & Letters, Gianthology, The Boston Compass*, and *New England Review of Books*. They were born and live in Cambridge, Massachusetts.

Fanny Howe has written many books of poetry, fiction, and essays. She was a Finalist for the Man Booker International Award for fiction. Her new book of poems, *Love and I*, from Graywolf Press, was published in Fall 2019.

Ben Mazer (b. 1964) was educated at Harvard University, where he studied with Seamus Heaney, and obtained his MA and Ph.D. at the Editorial Institute, Boston University, where his advisors were Christopher Ricks and Archie Burnett. He is the author of ten collections of poetry, including *Selected Poems* (MadHat Press, 2017), and the editor of several critical editions, including *The Collected Poems of John Crowe Ransom* (Un-Gyve Press, 2015), and *Selected Poems of Frederick Goddard Tuckerman* (Harvard University Press, 2010). Mazer lives in Cambridge, Mass., and is Co-Editor, with Raquel Balboni, of *Art and Letters*.

Wyatt Bonikowski's stories have appeared in *Atticus Review*, *Coffin Bell*, *Fairy Tale Review*, *Hobart*, *Necessary Fiction*, *New World Writing*, *Occulum*, *SmokeLong Quarterly*, *Wigleaf*, *Yemassee*, and others. He teaches literature and creative writing at Suffolk University in Boston, Massachusetts.

Meagan Masterman is a writer from Maine who now lives in Somerville, Massachusetts. She was shortlisted for the 2019 [PANK] Book Prize and the 2018 Metatron Prize. Her work has appeared in *Ghost City, Maudlin House,* and *Funhouse*. Find her on Twitter at @MeaganMasterman

Maria Pinto's prose has appeared in *Necessary Fiction*, *Word Riot*, and *FriGG*, among other journals, and she has been awarded fellowships by The Mastheads and The Writers' Room of Boston. When she's not ghostwriting or teaching at the literary nonprofit GrubStreet, she's in the woods looking for mushrooms. Her debut novel is in search of a home.

Jenny Grassl was raised in Pennsylvania, and now lives

in Cambridge, Massachusetts. Her poems appeared most recently in the *Boston Review* annual poetry contest, runner-up prize selected by Mary Jo Bang, and also in the anthology *Humanagerie* (Eibonvale Press, UK), *Ocean State Review*, *Rogue Agent*, and *Phantom Drift*. Her poems are forthcoming in *Rhino Poetry*, *Radar Poetry*, and *Massachusetts Review*.

Peter Brown's collection of short stories, *A Bright Soothing Noise*, won the Katherine Anne Porter Prize in 2010. With co-translators, he has published two books of poetry in translation, including *Elsewhere on Earth* by Emmanuel Merle and a French translation of the collected poems of David Ferry.

James Stotts is a poet living in Boston with his son. His first book, *Since*, was published in a second edition by Pen and Anvil Press. His second collection, *Elgin Pelicans*, is also from Pen and Anvil Press.

Susan Barba is the author of the poetry collection *Fair Sun* (David R. Godine, 2017). She works as a senior editor for *New York Review Books* and lives in Cambridge, Massachusetts. "Night Painting," "Summer Birth," and "Marathon" were previously published in *Fair Sun* (David R. Godine, 2017).

George Kalogeris is the author of a book of paired

poems in translation, *Dialogos* (Antilever, 2012), and of a book of poems based on the notebooks of Albert Camus, *Camus: Carnets* (Pressed Wafer, 2006). His current book of poems is *Guide to Greece* (Louisiana State University, 2018).

Tope Ogundare is a Nigerian currently living in Boston, and author of a poetry collection, *The Book of Pain*, published in 2018. His poems have appeared or are forthcoming from *Brittle Paper*, *Kalahari Review*, *Sentinel Literary Quarterly*, *Snapdragon*, *The Aquila*, *Pilcrow & Dagger*, *Moonchild Magazine*, *The Fable Online*, *Intima*, *Pangolin Review*, *Maple Tree Literary Supplement*, and elsewhere.

Fred Marchant is the author of five books of poetry, the most recent of which is *Said Not Said* (2017). Earlier books include *The Looking House, Full Moon Boat*, and *House on Water, House in Air*. His first book, *Tipping Point*, won the 1993 Washington Prize, and was reissued in a 20th anniversary second edition. Marchant has translated works by several Vietnamese poets, including Tran Dang Khoa and Vo Que. He has also edited *Another World Instead: The Early Poems of William Stafford*. An emeritus professor of English, he is the founding director of the Suffolk University Poetry Center in Boston.

Elke Thoms is a writer and stand-up comedian. Her poetry is featured in *City of Notions: An Anthology of*

Contemporary Boston Poems, *The Charles River Journal*, and was displayed in Boston's City Hall as part of the Mayor's Poetry Program in 2017. She studied English at Northeastern University, where she was the Editor-in-Chief of the university's literary arts magazine, *Spectrum*. Select poetry by Elke can be found on Instagram (@elkepoems).

Jennifer Barber's poetry collections are *Works on Paper* (The Word Works, 2016, Tenth Gate Prize), *Given Away* (Kore Press, 2012), and *Rigging the Wind* (Kore Press, 2003, Kore Press First Book Prize). Her poems have appeared in several anthologies and in the *New Yorker*, the *Missouri Review*, *Poetry*, *Poetry Daily*, the *Harvard Divinity Bulletin*, *December*, and elsewhere. A recipient of the Isabella Gardner Fellowship from the MacDowell Colony, she is the founding editor of *Salamander*, based at Suffolk University; she served as editor in chief from 1992 to 2018.

George Saitoh's fiction, essays, poetry, and drama have appeared in *Clarion*, *Aeqai*, *Kyoto Journal*, *Orbis*, *Word Riot*, *Santa Ana River Review*, *Janus Head*, *Gravel*, *Literary Orphans*, and Empty Mirror. His plays have been performed in Tokyo and Dublin. His debut novel is *All The Dead Animals* (2018). He holds a doctorate from the University of York and teaches at Waseda University, Tokyo. He was born in Dublin and regularly spends time in Boston. "Jerzy the Composer" was previously published in Issue 16 of *Clarion* (Pen & Anvil Press).

Meia Geddes is the author of *The Little Queen* and *Love Letters to the World*. She holds a Bachelor's degree from Brown University and Master's degree from Simmons University's School of Library and Information Science, and has been the recipient of a Fulbright grant to South Africa.

Liz Sux, aka Liz Bolduc, is an autobiographical cartoonist based in Boston, Massachusetts who catalogues books at a library during the day and inks comics by night. While Liz doesn't actually suck—they definitely like to use comics as a way to process internal anxiety as well as reclaim childhood memories and every day events. Please send all vegan doughnut recommendations or hate mail to lizbolducsux@gmail.com or say hello @Liz_Sux on social media.

Pınar Yaşar is a writer and instructor from Boston, MA. She holds a B.A. in English and has been published in *Haverthorn*, *La Bruja Roja*, *Cyberhex Press*, and *The Cannon*. The child of two immigrants whose marriage brought along with it generational trauma and racialized socialization, Yaşar writes about the Kurdish diaspora and records her family's legacy of leadership and loss through what she considers to be insurrectionist poetry.

Stephen Sturgeon is the author of two books of poems, *Trees of the Twentieth Century* (Dark Sky Books, 2011) and *The Ship* (Digraph Press, 2014). The two were collected and published in a single volume by Madhat Press in 2015.

Nate Klug is the author of *Rude Woods*, a modern translation of Virgil's Eclogues (The Song Cave, 2013), and *Anyone*, a book of poems (The University of Chicago Press, 2015). He grew up outside Boston and currently lives in the Bay Area of California.

Stephanie Burt is Professor of English at Harvard and the author of several books of poetry and literary criticism, among them *Advice from the Lights* (2017), as well as a regular contributor to the *New York Times Book Review*, the *London Review of Books*, and other journals in the US, UK, and New Zealand. Her new book of prose, *Don't Read Poetry: A Book About How to Read Poems*, will be published by Basic Books in May 2019.

Cassandra de Alba is a poet living in Massachusetts. Her chapbooks *habitats* (Horse Less Press, 2016) and *ORB* (Reality Hands, 2018) are about deer and the moon, respectively, and *Ugly/Sad* was released by Glass Poetry Press in 2020. She is a co-host at the Boston Poetry Slam at the Cantab Lounge and an associate editor at Pizza Pi Press.

Sarah O'Brien is a writer and artist from Woburn, MA. She earned her MFA in Writing from the University of Nebraska. Sarah is the Founder and Editor-in-Chief of the literary journal *Boston Accent Lit*. She is the author of the poetry book, *Shapeshifter*. She also wrote two chapbooks: *Moon-Soaked* and *Dancing on a Dead-End Street*. For more of her work and wit, visit sarahobrien.org, and follow her on social media @fluent_saracasm.

Katia Kapovich is a bilingual poet, originally from Moldova, who has been living in the US since the mid-1990s. She is the author of a dozen Russian poetry collections, of two volumes of short fiction in Russian, and of two volumes of English verse, *Gogol in Rome* (Salt, 2004) and *Cossacks and Bandits* (Salt, 2008). In Russia, she has received the prestigious Russian Prize twice: for fiction in 2013 and for poetry in 2015. Her original English language poetry has appeared in the *London Review of Books*, *Poetry*, *The New Republic*, *Harvard Review*, *The Independent*, *The Common*, *Jacket*, *Plume*, and numerous other periodicals, as well as in several anthologies including *Best American Poetry 2007* and *Poetry 180* (Random House). She was the recipient of the 2001 Witter Bynner Fellowship from the U.S. Library of Congress, and a poet-in-residence at Amherst College in 2007. She co-edits *Fulcrum: An Anthology of Poetry and Aesthetics* with her husband, the poet Philip Nikolayev.

Ryan Napier is the author of *Four Stories about the Human Face* (Bull City Press, 2018). He lives in Cambridge, Massachusetts. Follow him at ryannapier.net and on Twitter (@ryanlnapier).

Porsha Olayiwola is a writer, performer, educator, and curator who uses afro-futurism and surrealism to examine historical and current issues in the Black, woman, and queer diasporas. She is an Individual World Poetry Slam Champion and was named by GK100 as one of Boston's Most Influential People of Color. Olayiwola is the current poet laureate for the city of Boston and her first full collection of poetry is forthcoming with Button Poetry in November 2019.

Printed in Great Britain
by Amazon